USING WRITTEN SOURCES
in Primary History

Joan Blyth and Pat Hughes

Hodder & Stoughton

A MEMBER OF THE HODDER HEADLINE GROUP

British Library Cataloguing in Publication Data

A catalogue entry for this title is available from the British Library

ISBN 0 340 673761

First published 1997
Impression number   10 9 8 7 6 5 4 3 2 1
Year   2000   1999   1998   1997

Typeset by Wearset, Boldon, Tyne and Wear.
Printed in Great Britain for Hodder & Stoughton Educational, a
division of Hodder Headline Plc, 338 Euston Road, London NW1
3BH by The Bath Press, Bath,

Contents

List of sources and maps

Some sources are not contemporary but were specially prepared for this book. These are marked with an asterisk.

These maps are meant to help to explain parts of the chapters and sources to teachers. It is not expected that they will be used unaltered with children, though they can become the basis for classroom work as and when teachers think fit.

Acknowledgements

In the preparation of this book, acknowledgements are due:

To Hertfordshire County Council, and to Susan Flood of their Record Office, for the illuminated capital E on the cover and for Source 1; to the British Museum for the Rosetta Stone Photograph; to Jeremy Smith, of the Guildhall Library, for Sources 3 and 4, and Alison Derrett of the Royal Archives, Windsor, for Source 6, and for their interest and encouragement; to James Howarth, for Source 8; to Mike Hardman and the Grosvenor Museum, Chester, for Sources 10 and 10A and for advice about it; to Harmondsworth Press for Source 9; to J. M. Dent and Sons for Sources 11, 12, 13, 14, 15 and 16; to Bodley Head and BBC Publications for Source 17; to Basil Blackwell for Sources 2, 18 and 23; to Walter Scott Ltd for Source 19; to John Howell, San Francisco, for Source 20; to the Marquis of Salisbury for Source 21; to the Harvester Press for Source 22; to Thames and Hudson for Sources 24 and 25; to Frederick Muller for Source 26; to Jo Lawrie and Sevington School for Sources 27 and 28; to Manchester University Press for Source 29; to Ian Allan for Sources 30 and 31; to Bill Gaskell for advice about the Railway Races; to Mandarin Books for Sources 32 and 33; to Peugeot Motor Company and the National Motor Museum for Source 34; to Robson Books for Source 35; to Pavilion Books for Source 36; to Cwmbran Development Corporation for Source 37; to Torfaen Borough Council and especially to Heather Myers for advice about Cwmbran in recent years; to Gower Publishing Co. for Source 38; to Nene College Publications for Source 39; to Sylvia Collicott, for advice and help; to the *Scotsman* for Sources 41 and 42; to Ian Watson, Information Services Manager, Caledonian Newspapers Ltd, for references to the Erksine Bridge; to Barry Colford, Civil Engineer, for further advice about recent bridges; to Roy Loveluck, retired engineer, for advice and for drafting an illustration for the cable-stayed bridge in Source 40; to Lancashire County Museum Service for Sources 43, 44 and 45; to David Chadwick, Education Officer, Museum of Lancashire Textile Industry, for further advice about the Helmshore Mills; to Rodale Press for Source 46; to Chester City Record Office for Source 47; to Cheshire County Record Office for Source 49 and to Mrs E. M. Green, Archivist, for help in interpreting it; to Essex Record Office for two documents in the Appendix; and to members of staff of Record Offices for their kind co-operation in sending information about their own work, as reported in the Appendix: Ian Mason (Essex); David Bond (Hants); James Turtle (Gloucestershire) and Mary Mills (Wolverhampton).

Thanks are also due to Wendy Spalton and the staff of the Education Library, University of Liverpool, and to the history team at Liverpool

Hope University, particularly Kath Cox and Gill Goddard. The authors would like to thank the pupils and staff of Prescot County Primary and Longview County Primary. We would also like to thank the staff of the Cheshire County Council Library, Chester, and to Anna Clark and Lisa Hyde of Hodder and Stoughton Educational, for their patient help and advice.

Above all, we want to thank Alan Blyth (another 'Primary Bookshelf' author) for his interest, initiative, hard work and many contributions, including researching and sketching the maps and writing the Epilogue.

Joan Blyth
Pat Hughes
October 1996

Written sources and historical thinking

PURPOSE OF THE BOOK

The purpose of this book is threefold.

- Firstly and probably most obviously to help primary teachers access useful and relevant written source material for their history teaching.
- Secondly to show how verbal evidence, in a written format, can be used to promote successful history teaching and
- thirdly, to help to maintain the presence of history teaching in the primary curriculum, at a time when, like Geography, it is not entirely secure.
- Finally, to show how history teaching can inform good practice in English teaching.

Many teachers concerned with planning primary history have recognised the importance of using original sources throughout the primary years. But some of the existing collections of source material have been designed for secondary pupils and are often too lengthy and difficult for younger children. This book, a companion to Joan Blyth's *History 5 to 11* also in the 'Primary Bookshelf' series, has been written in order to provide something more suitable for the primary school.

As the chapter titles show, the book has been written with both the language (English or Welsh, where appropriate) and history curriculum principally in mind, though it is also relevant to other curriculum areas. The Final Report from the History Working Group published in 1990 has an excellent chapter on the relationship of history to the rest of the curriculum, which has not dated.

The examples chosen in this book refer to all kinds of 'words from the past', although a detailed examination of the importance of words from non-European cultures is not covered. Our examples are intended to offer different points of view, and to refer to different periods and regions, though with an emphasis – some might say too much emphasis – on England.

It is probably in England that the potential threat to primary history is most evident. Scotland, Wales and Ireland have their own histories and have been more vigorous about keeping these alive in schools and active in the defence of the stories of their communities. We hope to emphasise that an important means of anchoring the development of history in primary schools is by showing how closely it is linked with the development of literacy, whose position is secure. There is a tendency for the English content of the history curriculum to be taken for granted, so in this book we also look at how good History teaching can support literacy.

DIFFERENT FORMS OF HISTORICAL WRITTEN SOURCES

Numbers in this chart refer to sources from thepast reproduced in this book.

Personal records

- letters   18, 20, 21
- diaries and journals   2, 5, 6, 26
- scrapbooks
- notebooks
- diagrams
- certificates
- inventories   **49, and in the Appendix**
- wills
- house plans
- bills
- school reports
- ration books, identity cards etc.

Local records

- school records   28, 29
- street names
- place names
- directories
- parish registers
- maps
- guide books   19, 47
- local newspapers and periodicals   30, 31, 41, 42
- census returns
- local history pamphlets and collections of archive materials
- local government publications   37

Cultural and aesthetic

- Historical stories
- poems   17
- nursery rhymes
- songs – hymns, folk-songs, music hall, songs of protest
- plays
- recipe books
- advertisements   8, 34
- magazines

Government records

- census – local and national
- national and regional maps
- reports of commissions   18, 23
- Parliamentary papers
- Acts of Parliament
- Royal documents   1
- official statistics

Non-fiction texts

- reference books
- non-fiction accounts   11, 16, 22, 24, 25, 27, 33, 34, 36, 37, 40, 41, 46, 47
- CD-ROM

Non-paper writing

- papyrus
- brasses
- plaques
- clay tablets
- architecture
- art   3, 4 (engravings)
- coins
- samplers and quilts
- war memorials   10a

ORGANISATION OF THE BOOK

It is impossible for a book like this to look at each type of source in detail. For this reason we have chosen to look at specific written sources which we feel are representative of documentary sources in a particular period and so provide a chronological pathway of written source material through the ages. Only British sources are considered.

In Chapter 2 we will examine some of the recent evidence about how young children learn about the past and how written source material can be used to enhance this learning. In Chapter 3 we look more specifically at how documentary sources can be used at Key Stage 1. Chapters 4, 5, 6 and 7 look at written sources for particular periods in British history. These chapters include formal records, diaries, newspaper reports and letters. They also examine how the print on certain artefacts can also be used as an important written source. Chapter 8 provides some examples of how written sources can be used in local history, and extracts have been chosen which are less readily available to schools than the well-used directories and census returns. Each chapter from 3 to 8 is prefaced by a timeline of sources used.

Literature is another source of evidence about the past. In many of the fictional texts of writers such as Charles Dickens and Charles Kingsley there are vivid descriptions of Victorian Britain as seen and experienced by the writers themselves. These are good sources for learning about particular aspects of the past. Like all sources they need to be used with care, but they still form a valid source of evidence about the past. Such sources are discussed at the end of Chapter 6 in 'Victorian Britain'.

Chapter 9, on historical fiction, looks at how contemporary fictional stories about the past can be used to develop children's understanding and knowledge as well as engage their interest about the past. Historians have often been anxious and sometimes critical about the use of historical fiction as a source of evidence, but in this book we argue that good historical fiction can be a useful source of evidence and in Chapter 9 show how it can be used both for effective history and English teaching.

Written historical source material also includes secondary sources such as textbooks, CD-ROM and non-fiction texts. Chapter 10 looks at the use of secondary source material in primary schools and shows how history can support children's use of non-fiction texts. In this chapter the strong links between history and English are explored with a plea that reading and writing skills in English are not taught out of context. The book ends with a short Epilogue, indicating how written sources could figure in the teaching of history other than British.

HOW TO USE THE BOOK

History and English co-ordinators might like to read the whole book as it offers subject knowledge in a specialist area for both of them. The Introduction and Chapters 2, 9 and 10 will be most relevant for English co-ordinators as they show how the use of fiction and history non-fiction texts can inform and develop good primary practice in English teaching. Key Stage 1 teachers should find Chapters 2, 3 and 10 most useful. Key Stage 2 teachers should find Chapters 4 to 10 most helpful, depending on which particular study units they are teaching.

Using historical written sources to promote English teaching

Reading

- Skill in reading written sources of increasing complexity
- Familiarity with reading from a variety of different genres – diaries, letters, reports, newspaper articles
- Using texts which present challenging subject matter, providing an opportunity to extend children's thinking
- Using texts which contain figurative language and which have a variety of structural and organisational features
- Using a variety of non-fiction material (see chart Chapter 10, page 102)
- Reading myths, legends and traditional stories
- Examining classical literature
- Interpreting texts of increasing complexity

Writing

- Use written source material as models for their own writing – diaries, newspaper reports, narrative historical stories
- Identify in written source material characteristics of different kinds of writing (e.g. commentary, argument, narrative, comparison)
- Develop skills in using historical vocabulary in their own writing.

Speaking

- Skills in using written source material to explore, develop and explain ideas which the text identifies
- Using source material to investigate ideas about the world in which the children live both now and in the past
- Sharing ideas, insights and opinions based on use of written source material
- Reading material aloud and interpreting it for others through exposition, drama and role play
- Reporting and describing events and processes from the past using knowledge gained from historical sources
- Making comparisons between different forms of source material

Listening

- Listen to material read by others from written sources
- Develop skills in organising and reorganising material they have heard read aloud to ensure that they understand it and can identify key points
- Listen to the response of others to written source material and develop skills in questioning their response and extending and following up ideas which they have heard
- Listen and extend their vocabulary with historical language

USING WRITTEN SOURCES TO ASSESS LANGUAGE SKILLS

Historical written sources can be used as a means of recording and assessing children's language skills as well as their historical skills.

Reading

Once children begin to read the printed word their ability to interpret what they have read marks a further progression in their understanding, as does their ability to compare one text with another. In this book we argue and show how the use of written historical source material can provide a means by which children can develop higher order reading skills within a meaningful context – that is, within a history theme.

Assessing children's reading ability starts when very young children look at a simple text which may be supported by a picture (see Chapter 3) or be within a familiar environmental context such as a foundation plaque on a school wall. Initially children read the words, recall what they have read and answer simple literal comprehension questions on the text. At first these questions are oral questions which require a simple oral response, often one or two words. Later they become written questions requiring a written response.

Written responses to historical sources are a key feature in assessing children's understanding of the written word and the readability of the text or texts used. A quick glance through any English textbook containing passages for comprehension by older primary children shows a large number of historically-based texts for children to work on. Unfortunately these often have no historical context for the children for whom they are intended, and so children have difficulty in interpreting them because they do not have sufficient background information about that particular historical period.

Before children can respond to a text they need to form ideas about what they have read, to select words and organise ideas. In the early years these thinking processes are strongly supported by teacher input using words in the text and drawing on work already carried out about the theme. As children become more proficient and independent in reading and writing the historical sources can be used to provide models for creating sequences and organising phrases and sentences. When children read and use a number of different historical sources they can learn how different sentence structures are appropriate to different forms of writing.

As children become more able and confident readers their skill in understanding written source material extends and they can be encouraged to make inferences from the text. They will start in response to simple inferential questions, but will develop so that they can advance their own questioning skills to interpret a written passage. Children who have had good practice in using written sources throughout their primary years should be able to make an evaluative response to the text as well as make comparisons with other texts. The skills they develop are historical and linguistic.

Writing

Children's written response to historical sources will involve the transcription processes of physically writing, or word processing, spelling, punctuation, paragraphing and legibility. Composition of a text often involves using other texts as models. The list of different forms of historical written sources on page 000 demonstrates how many of these illustrate a variety of genres from which children may learn such as letters, diaries, journals, reports, recipes, advertisements, newspaper reports or non-fictional writing. In addition children's ability to create their own texts, such as devising a questionnaire for an oral history project, provides an indication of their growing maturity in using language to extract relevant information about the past.

The written source material chosen for this book is intended to extend children's reading, writing and thinking. Most of the extracts are followed by practical teaching strategies to show how this can be done.

Using historical written sources to promote learning of historical skills

Many of the activities in Chapters 3 to 8 use these skills.

Skills in chronology
- Reading and using basic historical vocabulary relating to time such as before, after, ancient, modern, BC, AD
- Using written sources to sequence events

Skills in extracting information to promote historical knowledge and understanding
- Reading progressively challenging historical texts
- Identifying different types of text
- Employing higher order reading skills such as the use of structural guiders to select relevant information
- Developing understandings of historical concepts such as change, past, democracy, empire

Skills in enquiry
- Asking basic historical questions
- Identifying ways in which answers to these questions may be found

Skills in interpretation
- Identifying the significance of a text and drawing inferences from it
- Making deductions from one or more written sources
- Recognising that written source material may represent a particular viewpoint and that evidence about the past needs to be collected from a number of different sources
- Assessing the usefulness and reliability of texts
- Distinguishing between primary and secondary sources and making use of them to support interpretations of historical events
- Recognising similarities and differences between the past and the present

Skills in organising and communicating information
- Ability to use the evidence collected to reach conclusions
- Communicate findings both orally and in written format using a variety of genres

CHALLENGES PRESENTED BY WRITTEN SOURCES FOR HISTORY AND ENGLISH TEACHING

Readability

Most written original source material in History was intended to be read by adults, although readability of texts is heavily influenced by whether the reader finds the text intrinsically useful or interesting. Beginning readers can often 'read' and certainly interpret their own personal written sources such as birth records, invitations and cards. However, even able primary children may have difficulties making sense of source materials which they can read but not necessarily understand. Texts vary in their degree of readability, structure, organisation and language.

Historical language has specialist words with which children need to become familiar in order to understand texts. Important historical concepts such as 'change' have many non-specialist

meanings which cause children difficulties in understanding when the same word is used in a historical context. This can be easily illustrated by asking children what a word such as 'change' means to them and let them provide a number of different interpretations. A class of 6 and 7 year-olds provided the following suggestions for 'change'.

Change
- change for PE
- change reading books
- changes in the weather
- ice cubes changing into water
- change for money in the newsagents
- using a rubber to change a word
- parent changing their hair colour

Only one of these suggestions really helps children if they are asked to describe the historical changes in two photographs taken of the same place over a number of years.

Identifying the historical meaning of everyday words is a challenging task and requires a good knowledge of children's levels of understanding about the world in which they live. Historical written sources usually assume prior knowledge. They often need more help and support than their ability to read the test itself might suggest. It is worth remembering that a source which may be difficult for a child to read can still be used as a stimulus for learning. Physically holding and looking through a Victorian family bible or a school log book provides a sense of the past even to the non-reader.

Reliability and bias

Once children can comprehend a text they need to move on to consider the reliability and bias of the source from which it has come. One simple way of doing this is to provide them with a series of true and false statements for a written source. After they have read the source or have had it read to them they can then say whether a particular piece of information is or is not contained within the source. Even comparatively young children can do this if the texts are taken from the very recent past – for example a report on a local soccer match written by a non-supporter, compared to a report on the same match written by a supporter of the local team. Children can be encouraged to ask who wrote a particular source and for what purpose. When did they write it? Were they present when the events took place? Is the information reliable and how can it be checked? The checklist below suggests some possible questions which children can be encouraged to ask of a written source.

Children and adults often have greater faith in the printed word than it deserves, learning how to use historical source material can help them to become more critical readers.

Ideally they should be able to reach some sort of conclusion about the evidence they have read even if the conclusion is 'not proven because of insufficient evidence'. Learning to live with uncertainty is one of history's most valuable lessons!

Asking questions checklist

1   What is this source?
2   What information does it provide?
3   When was it written?
4   Who wrote it?
5   Why did they write it?
6   Would the writer have first hand information about the topic?
7   Is the information reliable?
8   Can it be checked with any other source?
9   Where does the source come from?
10   Is it original?
11   Is it a copy?
12   How can we find out more about the source?

Language

Written source material, particularly early written source material, was frequently written in other languages and scripts. A class visit to the local grave-yard raises this issue very quickly as children struggle with Latin texts and Roman script. It is sometimes useful for children to see the original text, even when it is impossible for them – and often the teacher – to be able to read it. This is often most obvious when written source material is closely linked to artefacts and sources of non-paper writing such as the Rosetta Stone, the text on a Greek vase or a picture of an Egyptian tomb painting. Children then have an opportunity to see the actual script. It is less obvious when publishers have translated and printed scripts which were originally handwritten in another script and/or language. Even a printed Latin version of an extract from Tacitus about the Romans in Britain for example, looks very different from how the original script would have appeared. When children create texts with a quill pen or on a wax tablet and stylus or a school slate they can begin to have some empathetic understanding with the process with which the original author wrote. Sometimes it is helpful for children to look at the original alongside a transcript (see Sources 10 and 10A in Chapter 5 and Sources 48 and 49 in Chapter 8).

The accuracy of transcription from an original text is clearly an issue for historians, particularly when the original no longer exists. Older juniors attempting to copy from original sources may discover this for themselves when they return to the classroom after transcribing gravestones or wall plaques from a local church.

Interpretation of sources by writers

When writers of most modern primary school history texts use original documentary sources they edit them carefully so that they are short, pertinent and can be easily read by children. This may sometimes alter or distort the original sense of the text. As children move through the primary school such texts can be used as models for evaluation and contrasted with other extracts. The role of the writer and editor of a modern text can be discussed, as well as the actual text presented. The final chapter on the use of secondary material takes this up in greater detail and provides some suggestions for helping children to become critical readers of written sources of information.

PLANNING FOR USING WRITTEN SOURCES

In history the use of written source material will show itself in medium and short-term plans. Short-term planning may include specific history learning objectives related to the use of written sources, but these should not be the primary focus of all History lessons and activities as it distorts the process of learning History. Children's skill in engaging in historical enquiry is developmental and medium-term planning needs to reflect progression in use of written source materials.

The amount of time allocated to History varies from class to class and from school to school.

SCAA's booklet on 'Planning the Curriculum at Key Stages 1 and 2' provides four examples of History time allocation varying from 34 hours a year in a Year 1 class to 51 hours in a Year 6 class. SCAA guidance suggests an average of 1 hour per week at Key Stage 1 for history and 1.25 hours per week at Key Stage 2. The English curriculum is allocated a much greater share of curriculum time, averaging 6 hours per week in infant schools and 5 hours per week for older pupils. English should not be taught in a vacuum and subjects such as History, Geography and RE can be linked closely to it, so that English skills, knowledge and understandings about language are learnt within a meaningful and interesting context.

In English the use of non-fiction texts, familiarity with a variety of genres, and the children's use of them as models for their own writing, may appear in the long-term planning programme, as well as in the medium- and short-term plans. The SCAA booklet shows how the time-allocation for History can be used flexibly through a combination with English thereby also bringing out the ways in which the two subjects are related.

It is also likely that the use of historical written sources will appear in the medium- and short-term planning of other areas of the curriculum. A historical topic can be linked with Geography, when children are using maps as written historical evidence. In order to understand maps from the past children often need to make references to maps of the same area today. They are using specific geographical skills in the use of maps and historical skills to interpret the map as a historical source. The example on page 23 of the SCAA booklet indicates how history should be linked with Geography in local studies. In IT the use of CD-ROMs as a source of information can be linked with overall IT planning.

From these sources busy teachers should be able to select material suitable for their own classes, and to supplement that material from the suggestions in the appendices, or from their own resources. In general we do not specify the age-groups (within each Key Stage) for whom any particular extract is suitable, though sometimes we have. However, the material as a whole should provide a comprehensive range of historical source material, so that by the time children leave primary school they will have had extensive experience in the use of such sources.

The actual organisation of classroom work is given some attention. But the comments in the various chapters are not intended to suggest the way in which the work should be conducted. For one thing, much more attention should be given in practice to chronology, historical knowledge and understanding, interpretations of history, historical enquiry and organising and communicating historical findings. There is a need to tie together any scheme of work with a time-chart or time-line, especially when a long period of time is concerned (Romans, Saxons and Vikings). Time-lines of the selected sources are placed at the beginning of Chapters 3 to 7.

No doubt scholars with expertise in the various periods and topics we have included could each have suggested something more vivid, more representative or more up-to-date. We welcome that. For we are not specialists, except in what primary History requires and in what teachers need. We hope that our collection of sources will inspire new collaboration between the academic and educational worlds.

Starting points

HISTORY IN THE EARLY YEARS

The introduction of the National Curriculum has produced an emphasis on what children should learn and how it can be planned for, recorded and assessed. This has drawn attention away from the question of how children learn, both in the generic sense but also in a more subject-specific way. Determining what children should learn in the absence of understanding *how* they learn is dangerous, particularly when decisions have been informed by political rather than educational discourses. The question of what historical knowledge children should be aware of has been particularly susceptible to this debate. A heavy subject content turns us back to the Victorian philosophy of seeing the child as an empty vessel waiting to be filled. Experienced teachers know only too well the pitfalls of adopting this approach to their teaching.

Against this background there have been two distinct, but not necessarily separate, approaches to exploring how very young children learn History. There has been the research-led approach where writers such as Blyth (1988, 1989, 1994), Cooper (1992, 1995), Harnett (1993), and Lynn (1993) have researched the ways in which young children learn History and used their findings to recommend teaching strategies. Susan Lynn, for example, investigated how children began to consider the possible feelings and thoughts of people in the past who made and used the pictures, artefacts, buildings and documents which the children were studying. She

concluded that discussion, both with and without the teacher present, was an essential element in helping early learners make deductions and inferences from the source materials. Penelope Harnett (1993) looked at how children's progress in history could be assessed using visual sources.

These research findings have sometimes, but not always, informed the second approach to early years History teaching. This is a commercial one which has operated through published materials. Teachers' guides in primary history publications from Folens, Ginn, Heinemann, Longman, Oxford University Press, Scholastic and Simon and Schuster have helped teachers to identify historical skills and concepts in the work they already carry out with children and have produced resources to build on and extend this activity. These published materials have almost acted as the carrot to teaching History in the early years and can be contrasted to the stick of OFSTED inspections which have ensured that most schools now have in place comprehensive history and English policies and curriculum plans with long-term, medium-term and short-term objectives for their pupils.

Aspects of History have been identified by those planning the early years curriculum. In the nursery historical concepts, skills and knowledge have been recognised in tasks given to children, in stories told and during visits. The proposed desirable learning outcomes for children's personal and social development involve them in understanding themselves and others as well as extending their knowledge of the world. History provides a foundation for this understanding (SCAA, 1996).

RESOURCING HISTORY IN THE EARLY YEARS

Resourcing history teaching has often been more problematic than planning for it, particularly in the early years. This is because of the expense of providing resources such as artefacts in sufficient quantity to ensure that young children gain a concrete understanding of the past through physical objects. Written and visual source material is much cheaper, but published resources have often concentrated on photocopiable materials which seek to replicate the original source material. Big Resources Books (Ginn, 1993; Oxford University Press, 1993) and poster packs (Longman, 1992, 1996) provide a more attractive picture of written source material than the photocopiable sheets, but cannot replace the excitement of physically touching an original source, which then becomes an artefact as well as documentary evidence about the past.

If children can hold a school log book from the last century and turn its pages this is immensely more satisfying than working from a photocopiable sheet showing an extract from the same book. The photocopiable sheet can record the children's understanding of the historical evidence provided by a school log book, but children need the practical experience of touching, feeling and smelling it to ensure a deeper understanding of a school log as a historical source of evidence. This enables them to raise historical questions about the documentary source which may not be obvious from a photocopiable sheet – questions which may arise from curiosity about the book itself, the condition it is in, the type of handwriting inside it and the additional pieces of paper that may fall out of it. This makes history a much more practical and exciting activity.

In this chapter we look at ways in which very young children can be alerted to the written historical source material of their daily lives. It differs from Chapter 3 on documentary source materials for Key Stage 1 because it is concerned with the importance of identifying sources in the environment surrounding the child as a starting point.

We recognise that some children will enter school with a rich background knowledge of the importance of written sources as evidence about what happened in the past, while other children may be relatively unaware of print in their own or other's lives.

WRITTEN SOURCES IN THE EARLY YEARS

History provides a context for our lives. Our own personal history is a narrative, with a beginning, middle and an end, both fixed in time and place. Young children have their own history. This starts with the immediate recall of events which have just happened, to being able to discuss what happened yesterday, last year and when 'I was a baby'. Articulate pre-schoolers can recall what they have just done, and children can talk about periods in the past which they cannot recall at first hand but about which they have been told (such as a parent's own school days or summer holidays). As children retell and record their histories to others it becomes a more formalised and remembered past of their own. The daily oral news session moves on to written recording in a news book, describing what has happened the previous day, on a school trip or during the holidays. The distinction between what can be remembered at first hand and what has been reported by others can often become blurred and some children can retell events about which they could not possibly remember.

Children's personal sense of time starts with oral history, often supplemented by artefacts and visual sources such as photographs and video film. This oral history is what they supply themselves, as well as that of the people around them. The importance of the written source is often ignored or forgotten, although children may be led back to the past by looking at photograph albums with captions or titles such as 'Baby Album' or 'Holiday Snaps 1990–1995'.

Teachers often build on this by photographing children undertaking various activities during the course of the term and then displaying the photographs with suitable captions.

If children are to become independent learners in the school context, they will need to develop understandings of the written word as an alternative source of information to the spoken word. It is all too easy for children (and adults) to be 'print blind' – to ignore the print in the environment and so be unable to use print to find out more about themselves and the world. This chapter points to some of the areas in which printed source material exists, but may be ignored, forgotten or taken for granted.

EARLY WRITTEN SOURCES

1 Family histories

Families talk about their past and present. Taking photographs is often a means of making a visual record of activities and events which individual family members or a family group has undertaken. In some families these are organised in particular ways, so that it becomes easier to sort and find the pictures. A baby album can record the very start of a child's life. Today these can even include photographs of life before birth with photographs from hospital scans. The albums can be commercial or simply put together as a scrap book. They often contain writing to identify different times and places (such as captions) as well as an identifying cover with a name.

Some baby albums contain room for other forms of documentary evidence which were taken when the child was born, such as a certificate with the child's birth length and weight and a wrist band with the child's name. Other written source material collected soon after the birth of a child can include the birth certificate, a newspaper announcement of the birth, birth congratulations cards, a clinic book and even junk mail for baby products. Mothers who keep diaries may have a

diary record of the days and weeks immediately following the birth of a child.

The writing by baby photographs becomes a written source and adds to the visual evidence in a variety of different ways. Children can also enjoy 'reading' another child's baby album even if they do not have one themselves. Picture books such as *Grandma's Bill* by Martin Waddell and *Grandpa's Slide Show* by D. Gould provide a narrative for these sorts of activities, so that children both familiar or unfamiliar with looking at photographs from the past can see how this is part of a ritual.

(For a detailed Bibliography of all books mentioned in the text, turn to p. 129.)

Young children are often unknowing participants in on-going record keeping from the moment they are born. They attend hospital, doctors and dental appointments made for themselves or for their parents and their siblings. How much sense they make of these activities will largely depend on the ability of the adult with them to interpret what is going on. Standing at the receptionist's desk to record the appointment can be made into a meaningful activity when the parent lifts the child above the desk to see and hear what is going on. The sense of record keeping may be completely missed, or it may be incorporated into the child's understanding of the world in which they live.

Young children may also come into contact with written historical source material through their faith and the cultural practices of their family and community. A child attending a church each week may, as part of their weekly routine, visit the graves of past members of the family as do many visitors to graveyards. They look at and will be read inscriptions on gravestones and receive some understanding of their family history as well as an expectation of their own future. They may become familiar with the ritual associated with readings from a religious text, learning to say particular responses and react to some words in a particular fashion. The ways in which their community looks at and respects the written sources of its faith will provide models for their own behaviour.

Family events such as births, marriages, anniversaries and deaths are often associated with other written source material in the form of cards, letters, invitations, menus and bills. There is no form of base-line testing to indicate the quality of this type of experience individual children have prior to entering school. So teachers generally assume that most children have only a limited awareness of their own history and plan ways in which they can become involved in finding out more about their lives. This is often done through topics such as 'ourselves', where the historical aspect examines children's own history. It can never be as rich an experience as that provided by a child's own family because the teacher does not have access to the resources or information about every child's history. In order to overcome this teachers often share their own history with children. This allows for much greater detail, insight and knowledge and means that teachers can share and explain written source material arising from it (such as degree certificates).

The children's personal history is often recorded via time-lines, when children are invited to bring in artefacts, written sources and photographs to make a time-line of their own, or link in with a more generalised class display which looks at how children have changed since they were babies. Teachers often write captions to elaborate the source of evidence brought in and this in turn becomes a written source of evidence.

2   School histories

Nurseries and classrooms
Schools not only have a rich documentary history but also actively create one around the children in their care. Early years children become a part of this even before they set foot in the building. Children's names are entered on an admissions register for entry to school and children can be shown this later in their school career. Once they arrive in school they are placed on school registers and their presence in school is noted once or twice a day. The register informs about the present, but it also records past attendance as well as the names and sometimes the addresses of all those in a particular place at a particular time. Other records such as dinner registers, book clubs and library cards may be kept publicly so that children can see written source material in the process of being made.

The purposes for these activities should be identified and discussed, so that even very young children can become aware of what is going on around them, even if they may not initially understand the purpose of it all.

During the course of the school year other written sources are created. These may be records the children create themselves, such as weekly diaries or more formally a record of achievement. School reports are another written source, particularly if kept over a number of years. Attendance, sports and academic certificates are other forms of written source material which the school may be creating. Very young children may take part in assemblies where these written records are given out and children applauded when they receive them.

In the classroom itself other written sources may include a weather chart which records weather over a week or month, a calendar which records days of the week and months of the year or a birthday chart. It is easy to forget that these very obvious features of an infant classroom are also very simple written historical sources.

Schools – written sources in administration and buildings
Schools are full of rich documentary source material. This can include school log books, photo albums and scrap books, news letters, school magazines, newspaper cuttings, concert programmes and letters home to parents. Children may take home current versions of these (such as newsletters) and over the years become aware that these record what is going on in school in the present, what has happened in the recent past and what is planned for in the future.

An environmental print search around the inside and outside of a school can be useful in helping children recognise the print around them and be used to build up a word bank of 'words around our school'. How many of us as adults fail to read the 'pull' and 'push' signs on doors, or note the difference between the letters presented vertically or horizontally? Seeing and holding such records helps children develop an understanding of record keeping in the present, so that they can use this understanding to inform their awareness and interpretation of more complex historical sources.

In both the past and present people used signs and symbols to communicate with each other because a simple sign was quicker to understand and could be read by people who spoke different languages as well as by people who could not read. When children note and record signs from around the school it alerts them to the messages intended for them as well as to others. A surprising number of these, such as memorials and plaques were designed to provide a message to them by people living in the past. Other messages from the past may only be intended to record events as part of a legal obligation (e.g. registers and log books). Older children could be encouraged to find signs and messages in the local area which give information with or without any writing to aid communication. This could be done as a homework task.

Children could record both the signs and the audience for whom the sign is intended. Outside school, for example, many of the signs are likely to be road signs intended for car and lorry drivers. There is a wealth of reading material to be found on billboards, notices and advertisements in supermarkets and garages. Children may be able to think of international signs such as that for the Olympics and logos for particular products such as drinks and fast food restaurants. These can be seen and 'read' by people speaking many different languages. The growth of the Greek and Roman empires produced similar challenges for written communication. The Rosetta Stone shown below is one known attempt to communicate a message in more than one language.

Looking at signs in this way provides an opportunity for children to develop skills in looking at the audience targeted for the message. The purpose for the sign as well as the particular way in which the sign is created marks a relatively easy way into examining other forms of written communication, the reasons for it and the audience for which it has been directed.

Children can then move on to a more systematic examination of other messages in their environment. These can be divided up into different categories such as large-scale written source material like advertisements on billboards and buses, posters, shop signs and graffiti. Smaller-scale written sources material might

The Rosetta Stone: Egyptian hieroglyphs, demotics and Greek script all carry the same message

research writing, transcribing, summarising and generally communicating their knowledge and understanding of the subject in a variety of ways.

Sadly reading has often been put down as a passive activity in early years ideology and contrasted to 'active learning', despite the fact that children's environment both inside and outside school is bursting with print. Environmental print awareness is identified in many of the newer reading schemes, which have illustrations containing environmental print. Unless children are using it in their everyday lives they will not only grow up blind to much of the written source material around them but also unaware of the purpose of most of it.

3   Local historical sources

The local environment is another area full of historical source material which is accessible to very young children. The name of their own school or nursery may be linked to a local street, place name or to a person. Local street names may form some sort of pattern relating to the area in the past. Castle Street, Mill Street, Corn Street and Railway Terrace may still exist long after the castle, mill and railway have disappeared. An environmental walk round the area gives children an opportunity to familiarise themselves with the area immediately by the school, identify different street names and raise questions about the reasons for particular names. The print on street furniture such as pillarboxes can be pointed out and children encouraged to identify and perhaps draw pictures of street furniture in their area.

Inscriptions on local memorials, monuments and statues can be examined and read out. Photographs can be taken so that the memorials can be re-examined in the classroom. Old pub signs are another written historical source which can provide clues for their original use as well as marking something about the history of the local area. They may recall local family names 'The

include that on the everyday products they wear and use – labels on clothes and footwear, writing on T-shirts and sweatshirts, print on food tins and packaging. Environmental print may be in more than one language, and in another script.

In the classroom written sources can be sub-divided into sources for the children themselves to read and into the documentary evidence they provide for someone else to read such as registers, the school log book and books in the staff library. Written sources in school often vary considerably from subject to subject. In mathematics for example children write in order to answer problems set for them. They interpret data through graphical representation, they estimate, they create databases and use written language to describe the properties of different shapes. In history this is continued through

Derby Arms', or local events 'The Rocket', famous people 'The Nelson Arms', or the existence of a coaching inn 'The Packhorse'. The visual clue on the sign often aids reading and can be linked with other geographical and language work on symbols and signs in the local environment.

4 Stories and rhymes

Traditionally nursery rhymes have formed an important part of children's culture. Reading specialists have emphasised their importance in helping children to learn to read. They stress the rhyme and 'on set' element of the words, but learning traditional nursery rhymes also presents children with historical vocabulary. Understanding what words such as 'Muffin Man', 'posies' and 'meadow' mean can be helped with the use of accompanying illustrations, but when nursery rhymes are treated as a topic for further study there is an opportunity to look in much greater detail at exactly what the nursery rhymes are about.

Picture books can form important source material for aiding children's understanding of complex historical concepts, and there is a detailed Bibliography at the end of this book. Books such as David McKee's *Two Monsters* and *Tusk, Tusk*, enable teachers to discuss different interpretations of history. McKee's two monsters wage war from two different sides of the same mountain, but eventually realise that their perceived differences are non-existent. Alison Catley's *Jack's Basket* and Philippe Dupasquier's *Our House on the Hill* provide written as well as

visual evidence about the passage of time, thus helping children develop a sense of chronology within a narrative context. Dupasquier's books on different sites such as a garage, airport, building site, railway station, harbour and factory, provide a narrative for changes taking place in one spot during the course of a day. Janet and Allan Ahlberg's *Starting School* records changes over one day, over a week, over a half-term and finally over a year.

The narratives – or written sources – are supported by visual material, but the text is an important source of information about changes taking place in environments and situations close to the children's own experiences. Picture books such as Galbraith's *Laura Charlotte*, Ober and Lewin's *Always Adam* and Sheldon's *The Whale Song* record adults talking about their own past in a fictional format. Waddell and Read's *Coming Home* touches on the heartache of leaving one's country of birth and going to live in another country. In this case it is the story of an Irishman living in America and his journey back to Ireland with his grandson. Together they visit the places the grandfather knew as a child and meets people he knew when he was younger. They return to America, knowing that the grandfather will never be able to 'come home' again, but the grandson resolves to return 'one day'. Gray and Ray's *A Balloon for Grandad* describes the sorrow of families separated by continents and provides a good context for discussing the historical reasons why families move and become separated from each other. The chapter on historical fiction takes up this aspect of picture books in greater detail.

CHILDREN'S OWN WRITING

When teachers explore written sources with children they build on and develop children's understanding of the purposes for writing. This can be important for many children who do not see much writing being undertaken outside

school. Their own writing therefore becomes the model for writing and as this is often 'for the teacher' the wider purposes for writing may be missed. The National Writing Project suggested teachers ask children to create a writing audit to see what writing took place in their own homes. The results from this showed that writing lists and letters were the most commonly observed models for writing and in the vast majority of cases it was women who were seen as writers. A writing audit can be an important way of identifying the base-line for children's writing experiences in their everyday life.

When children look at their own writing it raises issues about their purposes for writing as well as other people's reasons for writing. Questions raised here can later be raised again in helping children to interpret written source material, both contemporary and from the past.

to cover stories, notices, instructions, newspapers and even sample work for their own record of achievement. Children sometimes write for unknown audiences such as magazines, exhibitions and competitions. It is this very personal and limited experience of writing which they bring to the documentary historical sources they study. Words like 'diary' mean a daily or weekly diary they are asked to write for the teacher. The creation of famous diaries like that of Anne Frank, Queen Victoria (see Chapter 6, Source 26) and Samuel Pepys are histories in themselves. A diary may be used as a marker for future events and appointments. It may be a

Purposes for writing
- To remember things
- To communicate information and ideas
- To entertain, elicit a response, evoke an emotion
- To persuade
- Explore feelings

Interpretation of any written source involves questioning the purpose for a piece of writing. It also involves looking at the intended audience. Few children write for themselves, but written source material such as diaries or poetry may have been created just for the writer and not intended for a wider audience. This idea of personal writing may be very difficult for children to understand when they are asked to interpret an extract from a diary. Samuel Pepys wrote his diary in shorthand in a deliberate attempt to prevent others from reading it (see p. 21 in Chapter 3). It is partly for this reason that it makes such fascinating reading for adults today, although the censored extracts provided for children about the plague and fire of London must make them wonder why he was so secretive (see Chapter 3, Sources 2 and 5).

In school situations children often write for other children and adults in the school community. In fact the vast bulk of their writing is intended for this audience. This writing is likely

record of past events. A diary may have more than one author and history has often been recorded as a type of diary. Bede's *Ecclesiastical History* and *The Anglo-Saxon Chronicles* (see Chapter 4) could be looked at in this way. Children can be helped in their interpretation of written source materials if they understand something about the genre itself.

The writing process

The way in which a piece of writing is created today, raises important issues about how it was created in the past. Most of children's writing is done by hand, although some is typed up on a wordprocessor, either by children themselves or by an adult for display. The shortage of computers in primary classrooms means that the reality of using them as wordprocessors, rather than glorified typewriters, is still in the future. However most classrooms have plenty of paper and writing implements so the question of what to write on and with what does not occur to children. Looking at written sources in the remote past involves exploring not only the message but also the medium; such as the clay tablet, the brush, the quill pen and the slate.

History transmitted through writing and printing

Children's own experience of reading and writing needs to be built on in order for them to come to some understanding about the nature of written source materials. The history of writing and printing is a topic on its own. The beginnings of writing and the sort of materials used can be linked with who was able to write – and of course who was not able or allowed to write. So too can the impact of the invention of the printing press which meant that documents could be mass-produced.

If children have an opportunity to study writing in a pre-print society such as Ancient Egypt or Greece, they can then use this information to see how technological change has altered society in the past and continues to do so.

In order to interpret documentary sources from the past children need to explore and interpret writing carried out in their daily lives. If they have limited experiences these need to be extended.

In this chapter we have spent time exploring ways in which children can be taught how and why texts are created. This starts with texts they read themselves as well as with texts they create. This is clearly part of the English curriculum but can be linked with the History curriculum by looking at how and why texts have been created in the past. This involves looking not only at the purposes and audiences for such texts, but the format which they take.

THREE

Key Stage 1

Capital E 1588	Fire of London 1666	VICTORIA'S CHILDREN 1848	MAJESTIC II 1922

One of the triumphs of National Curriculum History, both in the 1991 and in the 1995 English Orders, was the official inclusion of history at Key Stage 1. For in spite of the possible threat to history as a subject at this Key Stage, a historical component must be maintained there, even in an integrated curriculum or in one which gives more prominence to English.

It may seem over-optimistic to expect teachers of infants to use written sources in history at all, in spite of their inclusion in both Orders. Yet it is possible to bring in genuine contemporary sources, especially in the familiar guise of pictures with writing on them, through stories read by the teacher and through children's books. Certain pictures and posters related to a particular time are just as relevant as books or papers. Examples might be the Bayeux Tapestry – one or two strange Latin words can be fun – and propaganda posters issued during World War Two.

The 1995 Order for Key Stage 1 emphasises, in the introductory panel, four aspects of history: an 'awareness of the past'; chronology; differences between past and present; and asking questions about the past. The Key Elements add to these: historical knowledge; communication (how children tell about the past in drawing and writing and many other ways); and interpretation of the past. Areas of Study designated to implement these are: family history, social history since 1945, periods of the past 'before living memory' (i.e. before 1900) and famous people and events in the past. In the rest of this chapter, four sources are suggested which may help in this ambitious but flexible Programme. Each chapter opens with a time line, as above, of the sources to be found there.

A DECORATED CAPITAL LETTER

The first example is Source 1, a single letter of the alphabet which the children will just have mastered: an illuminated capital E. It comes from a borough charter conferred upon Hertford in the late sixteenth century by Elizabeth I (the 'E' was hers). It celebrates the triumph over the Spanish Armada in 1588, which averted the danger of a Spanish invasion.

'Illuminated capitals' like this one were drawn and hand-painted by monks in monasteries in medieval times. By the sixteenth century, documents such as this Hertford charter were

Source 1 Illuminated capital from Elizabeth I's charter to the Borough of Hertford, 1588. Reproduced by kind permission of the Borough Council of Hertford

gaps between words. Some of the later lettering is *more* difficult to make out.

This 1588 document has been selected as contributing to topics 'beyond living memory'. In the original coloured document, the one on the cover of this book, the word 'Elizabeth' is painted in gold. The Queen is wearing her red robe edged with ermine fur which she wore on state occasions. On her head is her crown, and she is holding the orb (the spherical object) and sceptre, denoting royalty. She is shown sitting on a cushion with tassles on her throne, and with the Latin words 'Vivat Regina' (Long Live the Queen) above her. Those words would have given her no trouble, for she was a fluent speaker of Latin. The rest of the charter, also in Latin, expresses the thankfulness of the town of Hertford for the failure of the Armada and the popularity of the Queen. The Museum of London has a similar capital E, but dated 1559. It shows Elizabeth, aged 26, with flowing fair hair (see the Bibliography). This document could be the central interest for a story about the Armada, and children could be encouraged to 'read' the picture by question and answer. For example:

- How do we know if someone is royal?
- What do 'orb' and 'sceptre' mean, and why are they important?
- What is the Queen wearing round her neck? (i.e. a ruff)
- Have you seen any pictures of other people wearing anything like that?

A discussion of this sort could lead on to each child taking a letter of the alphabet and making a capital of his or her own, on a large piece of paper, for another famous person in history, with a few beautifully-written words afterwards (in English) worthy of the person. The capital should also be decorated with pictures and flowers and fruit, or whatever the child thinks appropriate. There could in the end be an exhibition of everybody's illuminated capitals on part of the classroom wall. Then each child could say what she or he had found out about their historical

being drawn up by lay clerks and scribes as well as by monks. Postcards showing illuminated capitals can be obtained quite easily from sources such as the British Museum, the John Rylands Library in Manchester and many cathedral bookshops. They are cheap, and easy for infants to handle. It is helpful if a teacher knows the name of the manuscript (and what it signifies); whether it was executed by a monk or a scribe, a lay scholar or a clerk; and if possible what actual word is begun by the illuminated capital and what other words follow. This information is sometimes, but not always, given on the back of the postcard itself. It should be remembered that medieval lettering is usually quite easy to make out, but it will be in Latin, with abbreviations, and sometimes without character. The teacher may need to suggest names. Or, if it seems more appropriate, a favourite contemporary character could be chosen instead.

THE GREAT FIRE OF LONDON, 1666

Story-telling and reading have always been a favourite method by which young children are stimulated to welcome information and ideas, particularly in the infant classroom. Sometimes it is better to have 'story-time' at the beginning rather than the end of an afternoon, so settling children down after the lunch break. This is a good time to teach about the past, especially 'ways of life before living memory'. The Great Fire of London is one of the most devastating, and best remembered, social events in English history. It raged from 2 September 1666 for five whole days, and the destruction can only be compared with the World War Two blitz on English cities. Almost three hundred years later, the massive bomb in Manchester on 15 June 1996 inflicted a traumatic effect on a whole city and, because of the instant transmission of news and images today, on the whole country. But in the days of the Great Fire of London, there was no separate 'central business district': central London was where many people lived, and in that sense the impact of the fire was more like that of the blitz. Indeed, there was a direct link in historical memory, for some of the new buildings put up after the fire were among those damaged or destroyed in the blitz.

Samuel Pepys, the diarist and Government official (Secretary for the Navy), portrays the drama of the fire in a simple and compelling way. The 1995 Order for History suggests that children should hear the words of an eye-witness to an event, and Pepys was certainly such an eye-witness. Children will probably not have heard before that he is pronounced 'Peeps'. Two sources are given from Pepys' diary, and two seventeenth-century engravings illustrate the London of the period. These show how written and pictorial sources help to explain each other.

September 2nd (Lord's day) . . . So I made myself ready presently, and walked to the Tower, and there got up on one of the high places, Sir J. Robinson's little son going up with me; and there I did see the houses at that end of the bridge all on fire, and an infinite great fire on this and the other side [of] the end of the bridge; which, among other people, did trouble me for poor little Michell and our Sarah on the bridge. So down with my heart full of trouble to the Lieutenant of the Tower, who tells me that it begun this morning in the King's baker's house in Pudding Lane, and that it hath burned down St Magnes Church and most part of Fish-street already, by London Bridge.

So I down to the water-side, and there got a boat, and through bridge, and there saw a lamentable fire. Poor Michell's house, as far as the Old Swan, already burned that way, and the fire running further, that in a very little time it got as far as the Steele-yard, while I was there. Everybody endeavouring to remove their goods, and flinging into the river, or bringing them into lighters [shallow river boats] that lay off; poor people staying in their houses as long as till the very fire touched them, and then running into boats, or clambering from one pair of stairs to another. And among other things, the poor pigeons, I perceive, were loth to leave their houses, but hovered about the windows and balconys, till they burned their wings, and fell down . . .

Source 2   Extract from Pepys' Diary, 1666 (quoted in C. R. N. Routh and R. Birley, *They Saw It Happen, 1485–1688* Oxford: Basil Blackwell, 1956, pp. 180–1)

Source 2 could be read with a class as far as the words 'London Bridge', where the first part ends. Pepys and his household were in bed asleep when

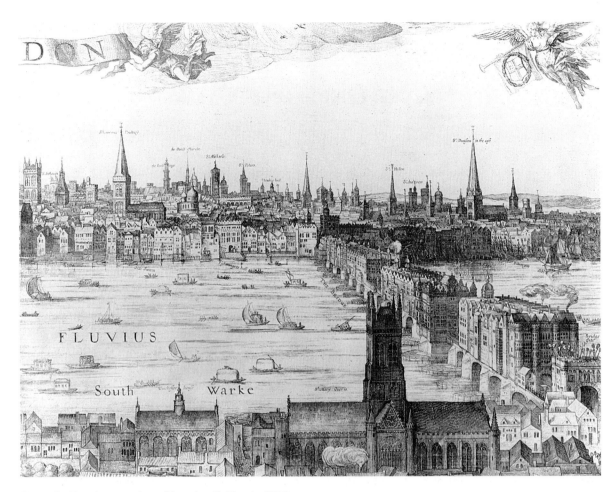

Source 3   Dutch engraving of London Bridge in 1616

Jane, one of his servants, woke him up with news of the fire. Pepys and his young friend climbed up the Tower of London and saw the fire threatening London Bridge where Sarah lived. She was the junior maid in his household, and 'Michell', whose house near the Bridge was burned, was Betty Michell, a friend of Pepys. When this part of the story is read, children may be asked where the Tower of London is, and what it is used for today: some may have visited the Tower. There could be discussion too of what people must have felt about the burning of three hundred houses in a much smaller city than London is today.

The second piece of teaching in Source 2 is about London Bridge as well as the fire. This part of the work could start by reading the rest of the source, from 'So I down to the waterside [sic] ...' to '... fell down'. London Bridge then had quite tall houses and shops, separated by short stretches of roadway, most of the way across. All except the gateways of the Bridge were built of wood, so Pepys would have been very worried about them. But because the strong wind which spread the fire blew from the east, it never reached beyond the stone gateway and the gap beyond it. (Each street to which the fire spread, at first, lay to the west of the one before: you can work that out by comparing the source with a street map of London today.)

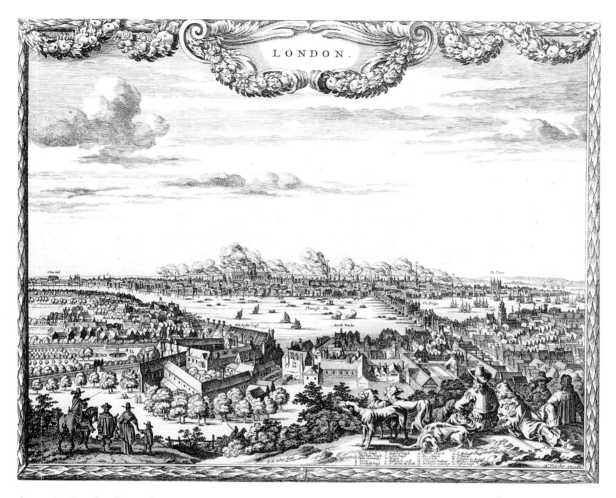

Source 4 'London Burned Down': part of a Dutch-engraved panorama, 1666

ENGRAVINGS OF SEVENTEENTH-CENTURY LONDON

Source 3 shows how a Dutch artist, N. Visscher, completed his engraving of the Bridge in 1616, just fifty years before the fire. It shows the wooden buildings and the stone gateway clearly, and also the various kinds of craft on the River Thames. He labelled all the main buildings, and it is just possible, with a magnifying glass, to make out some of the names.

Source 4 is another engraving by the same artist. It is part of a huge panorama of the whole of London which took him many years to complete. But this part has a title which means

'London Burned Down'. So somebody must have added the smoke and flames, after the fire. If you look carefully, you can see that there is another name, P. N. Schut, as well as Visscher's. So maybe it was Schut who added the 'fire' part to this copy of Visscher's engraving. He did not do it very well. For one thing, he knew that the wind came from the east, as we have seen, and he showed it that way; but Visscher's craft on the river had their sails filled by a *westerly* wind. You will also notice that there are no buildings actually on fire. All the same, the effect is gruesome enough!

SUGGESTED ACTIVITIES

All sorts of questions could arise from Pepys's description of what he saw:

- What happens today in the case of fire?
- Where was the fire brigade when the alarm was raised? Was there a fire brigade?
  Where were the police? Who did anything about the fire?
- Why were there so many boats on the River Thames, when people tried to get away from the fire? (In Charles II's reign, the River was one of the best ways of travelling through London)

Other questions could concentrate on the Bridge itself, especially if Sources 3 and 4 could be enlarged or projected:

- Smoke is shown in both pictures. What is the difference between the two kinds of smoke?
- What are those objects on top of the spikes on the bridge gate in Source 3?
- Why do you think that the fire did not spread across the bridge? (probable answer on page 22).
- Do you think that Source 3 is part of Source 4? (No: why?)
- What is the big difference between Old London Bridge and London Bridge today? (easier of course for children who know London)

For some children it might also be possible to ask:

- Why might the smoke and flames in Source 4 have been added to a picture made before the Fire?
- Which of the ships in Sources 3 and 4 would have been able to go under the Bridge?

Source 5 describes Pepys' visit to the Palace of Whitehall, where Charles II lived. Whitehall is now where many Government offices are: the Changing of the Guard takes place outside the Palace. (See Chapter 8 for the story of King Charles II before he was 'restored' to the throne.)

I go to White Hall, and there up to the King's closett in the Chappell, where people come about me, and I did give them an account [that] dismayed them all, and word was carried in to the King. So I was called for, and did tell the King and Duke of York what I saw, and that unless his Majesty did command houses to be pulled down nothing could stop the fire. They seemed much troubled, and the King commanded me to go to my Lord Mayor from him, and command him to spare no houses, but to pull down before the fire every way . . . At last met my Lord Mayor in Canning-Street, like a man spent, with a handkercher [sic] about his neck. To the King's message he cried, like a fainting woman, 'Lord! what can I do? I am spent: people will not obey me. I have been pulling down houses; but the fire overtakes us faster than we can do it'.

Source 5   Extracts from Pepys' Diary (The Readers' Library Publishing Co. edition, compiled by Metcalfe Wood, London: c.1936, p. 131)

The Lord Mayor of London, normally a very dignified and important official, is too overwrought to continue pulling down houses as the King had ordered. Many rich and important people lived farther from the centre of London and were able to accommodate the property of their city-centre friends who could move it in carriage or on boats, as Pepys himself did; but the poorer people had nowhere else to go or to take their things. They could only try to save at least some of their belongings on carts, much as refugees all over the world do today.

SUGGESTED ACTIVITIES

- Children could think why fire brigades today do not usually pull down houses.
- They could also imagine what it was like when all the people from houses caught up in the fire had to try to move out.
- They could think why the people would not do what the Lord Mayor commanded.
- They could perhaps go a little farther with this with some role-playing.

- They could try painting a big collective picture of the fire, with the bridge burning: each child could paint one house on fire or of one boat on the river, and they could all be put together. Source 4 can help here, but remember that it does not show any buildings actually burning.) They could use other visual sources to help them draw the houses.

QUEEN VICTORIA'S CHILDREN

Source 6 is about Queen Victoria's sketch of her children (see Chapter 2, p. 17). It is a rarely-seen depiction of her six eldest children and their three older German cousins. These cousins were the three tallest children; Eliza, Adelaide (Ada) and Feodore (Feo). Actually, they were the granddaughters of Queen Victoria's mother, the Duchess of Kent, by her first marriage. So they were really *step-nieces* of the Queen, and *step-cousins* of her own children. These nine children were all lined up in order of age and height to welcome the Duchess of Kent, who was grandmother to all nine of them, on her birthday

visit to their home at Osborne House, near Carisbrooke on the Isle of Wight, on 17 August 1848. It is said that they each held a 'nosegay' to present to the Duchess. But do they all hold flowers in the picture?

Osborne House had been bought by Victoria and her husband, Prince Albert, so that the family could get away from the noise and bustle of public life (see Source 26 in Chapter 6). While she was at Osborne House Victoria employed a 'drawing master', William Leighton Leitch, to give her sketching lessons. Victoria was so pleased with this row of children doing honours to her

Source 6 Queen Victoria's sketch of her six children and three step-nieces (from Duchess of York and Benita Stoney, *Victoria and Albert: Life at Osborne House*, London: Weidenfeld and Nicolson, 1991, p. 99)

mother that she made a quick sketch for her day's diary. It now remains in the Royal Archives at Windsor Castle. While she was away from London, she liked to sketch and paint and dance and to venture into the nearby sea from her 'bathing hut'. This impression of the Queen as a happy mother with her growing family is in stark contrast to her later and better-known solemn years after Prince Albert died in 1861.

SUGGESTED ACTIVITIES

Very young children can gain much from this family sketch. It gives a teacher the opportunity to tell a story about Queen Victoria, how she unexpectedly came to the throne in 1837 at the age of only 18 (and how long ago was 1837?), her adoration of Prince Albert, her happy family life, and her very long reign (1837–1901) – how long was that? Questions could be asked about the picture itself, such as:

- Do you think it shows that Mr Leitch was a good 'drawing master'?
- Why is Bertie in trousers, and not Alfred?
- What job do you think the lady did who is holding Louise, the baby?
- As the three tallest girls were the Queen's *nieces*, which of the other six was her eldest child, and which the youngest?
- One of the children's real names was Helena. Which one? (Prince Albert was German, and 'Lenchen' is a pet name for 'little Helena' in German.)
- Would you and your family stand in a row like this when your Gran comes to see you?

A more demanding question can be asked. Children could be told that the rule about 'succession' to the throne in our country is that:

- the eldest son succeeds – even if he has an older sister
- if there is no son at all, then the eldest daughter succeeds
- if there are no children, then the eldest nephew succeeds
- if there are no nephews, then the eldest niece succeeds

Victoria herself had become Queen because William IV, the king before her, had no children and no nephews.

- Which of Victoria's six children was likely to succeed her on the throne? (They all lived and so it was Bertie, who became King Edward VII.)

There could also be a general discussion about how our Queen Elizabeth II may be considering altering the rules of 'succession'.

Another activity, related to the family history called for by the Order, is that children could be asked to make a family tree: some may have done this already for their own families. First they would need to learn how a family tree is constructed, putting the eldest brother or sister on the *left-hand side* (whereas in Source 6 Victoria had arranged her family with the eldest on the

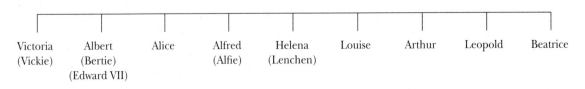

Victoria & Albert

| Victoria (Vickie) | Albert (Bertie) (Edward VII) | Alice | Alfred (Alfie) | Helena (Lenchen) | Louise | Arthur | Leopold | Beatrice |

Source 7 Queen Victoria's family tree (not a contemporary source)

right-hand side). Then they could be shown the diagram of Victoria's family tree in Source 7 and could spend quite a time making a fair copy of it. Further questions could arise from comparing the diagram with the sketch:

- Can you find all the people who are in the sketch?
- Can you find anyone who is not in the sketch? How can that be? Some people may want to add faces to their copy: the lack of likeness doesn't matter!

And to finish with, there could be general questions such as:

- Think what it would be like if you and your brothers and sisters, those who have them,

were to line up like Queen Victoria's children. Would the oldest one be:

the *biggest* one? And the *youngest* the *smallest?* Is there anyone's family where that is not true? But it was true of Victoria's family, wasn't it? Did that make it easier to draw the sketch?

This introduction to Victorian England could be developed, forming the basis of more stories about Victorian life (see Chapter 6) or children's fiction about life in the nineteenth century (see Chapter 10). In Key Stage 1 there is no constraint about historical periods: we can go where we want to.

WHITE STAR LINER

So far, in this chapter, the sources have illustrated the sixteenth century (a famous person, Elizabeth I), the seventeenth century (an important event as viewed by an eye-witness – Samuel Pepys) and the nineteenth century (children of Queen Victoria – a famous person). The final source represents a 'way of life' in the early twentieth century. It is mainly a poster representing a ship, but includes a few words too.

Source 8 is the *Majestic* White Star 'liner' in the 1920s, when the pinnacle of travel was sailing on this giant ship on the North Atlantic route. A journey from Southampton to New York took about five days, so when regular and cheaper flights taking only about five *hours* became available, that was the end of regular use for those liners. But sixty years ago they were in their prime. The wealthy and important people, including Prime Ministers and film stars, went first-class; but some others used the lower decks, including third-class passengers seeking work in the USA. All the White Star ships had flags with five-cornered white stars on a bright red background, like the one in Source 8. They also

had names ending in 'ic', including the *Titanic,* wrecked on an iceberg during her maiden voyage in 1912, when many of the third-class male passengers were drowned. The *Titanic* had been built, like most of her sister White Star ships and many smaller ones, by Harland and Wolff of Belfast, the world-famous shipyard in the north of Ireland.

But the *Majestic* had a more unusual beginning. She was actually under construction in Hamburg in Germany, when war broke out in 1914. She was to have been called the *Bismarck,* after the nineteenth-century German statesman. During the war she remained unfinished, but was completed just afterwards when Germany had been defeated. When the peace settlement was made, the Allied Powers made the Germans pay 'reparations' for the damage they had done, and as part of these reparations the *Bismarck* was completed and sent to Southampton in 1922, where she was fitted out and renamed *Majestic,* or really *Majestic II,* replacing an earlier White Star ship.

At that time, as the poster says, *Majestic* was the

Source 8 Poster advertising the White Star Line, c.1926 (from John S. Haworth, *James Howarth and Company*, London and Leicester: James Heworth Ltd 1989)

largest liner in the world, with a tonnage of 56,000. A modern oil tanker is about twice that size. But you could have fitted *four hundred* large eight-bedroomed houses into her space. Such luxury liners were called 'floating palaces'. Her first-class passengers enjoyed luxurious meals, a swimming pool nine feet deep and lined with marble, a cinema, a supervised children's playroom, a dance hall and suites of private rooms. Some liners had wide solid mahogany stairways made by skilled craftsmen. Many crew members were employed to look after the travellers in every possible way. When King George V and Queen Mary visited the *Majestic*, the royal standard was flown at her masthead. (Later, of course, Queen Mary had a liner named after her, but that was after the White Star Line had been joined with the Cunard Line.)

During the Second World War the big liners were painted grey and used as troopships. But the British commanders thought that *Majestic* was so big that, although she could have carried many soldiers, German bombers would easily find and destroy the ship and all on board. In any case she was getting old. So in 1939 she was taken to Rosyth, on the Firth of Forth, west of Edinburgh, to be burned and broken up. Her three funnels had to be cut off so that she could be towed under the famous Forth railway bridge. So *Majestic* arrived in England because of the World War One; became part of a new and more luxurious way of life between the two world wars; and ended her life because of the coming of World War Two.

SUGGESTED ACTIVITIES

Class discussion of the *Majestic* poster could include:

- meaning of the word 'Majestic': its links with 'majesty'. These words are all connected with 'major' or 'maior', the Latin for 'bigger'.
- meaning of 'liner' – a ship making scheduled sailings from one place to another (e.g. Southampton and Cherbourg to New York) as distinct from a 'coaster' which went from place to place taking its chance of a cargo. There were other 'lines' such as Cunard and P & O.
- purpose of the little ships (tugboats) in the poster. Why are they puffing out smoke and *Majestic* isn't? (Tugs were busy getting the big ship out of dock into position while she had not yet got up steam: also they burned coal while she was oil-fired and made less smoke).
- Where is Cherbourg? Why did *Majestic* call there? Trace her route to New York on the globe. Why is that better than following it on an atlas map?
- How did the passengers go on board, and leave, the ship?

- Rather than simply being told that part of the story, children could discuss how *Majestic* with her tall funnels could get beyond the Forth Bridge to Rosyth on her last journey.
- Liners are still used now for world cruises and other purposes when it is not necessary to travel quickly. Can you name any? (Queen Elizabeth II.) Who might travel on liners now? Do you think that a modern liner would have any kind of luxury that *Majestic* didn't have?

Activities might include:

- Make a red flag, and stick on a White five-pointed Star.
- Look out for posters on your way to school. What are they advertising? Are they for everybody, or only for the sort of people who might have sailed with the *Majestic*?
- Make a poster to encourage people to go on the sort of holiday you go on? How would that be different from the *Majestic* poster?
- Write a day in your diary as a passenger on the Majestic.

MAKING A TIME-LINE

Assuming all four topics are studied, a short time-line could be made by each child, modelled on the one at the beginning of this chapter. Alternatively, one big chart could be made on the wall, and pieces of work about each extract could be carefully inserted at the right place, with plenty of talk about why that is the right place and questioning to make sure that everybody understands. If they like, the children could add other events in the past that they have heard about. The children should then be reminded that all these events really did happen; that they happened long before 'now'; and that they happened in that order because we know the year when they took place.

In this way it becomes possible to reinforce learning about Key Stage 1 history, including the Key Elements. Many more ideas can be gleaned from two Government publications between 1991 and 1995 (see the Bibliography).

FOUR

Romans, Anglo-Saxons and Vikings in Britain

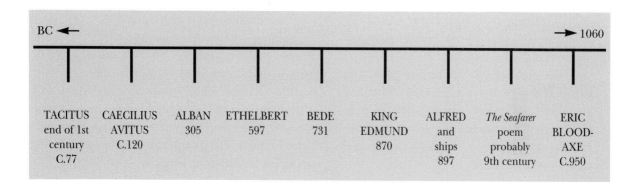

BC ←								→ 1060
TACITUS	CAECILIUS	ALBAN	ETHELBERT	BEDE	KING	ALFRED	*The Seafarer*	ERIC
end of 1st	AVITUS	305	597	731	EDMUND	and	poem	BLOOD-
century	C.120				870	ships	probably	AXE
C.77						897	9th century	C.950

Nine sources have been chosen for this first millennium AD (and a bit more). The relevant ones could be used in more detail for whichever part of the period is selected for closer study.

TACITUS AND BRITAIN

Source 9 is a translation of a passage originally written in Latin by Tacitus, a Roman historian writing near the end of the First century AD (see Chapter 1, p. 8). This passage comes from Tacitus' biography of his son-in-law Agricola, who was responsible for extending Roman rule further into Britain and for preventing any revolt. Tacitus himself was concerned to defend Agricola's reputation against his enemies in Rome, and so is prone to exaggerate his son-in-law's virtues; nevertheless we have reason to think that much of what he wrote gives a fairly accurate picture of early Roman Britain.

Agricola's view was that the Britons had been barbarians but had readily accepted Roman rule and benefited from it. But he recognised that not all the Britons agreed, for he had to account for Queen Boudicca's almost successful revolt in AD 61. We now also know, from excavations and artefacts, that many of the British tribes were led by chieftains who were sophisticated fighters capable of building fortifications such as Maiden Castle in Dorset. They had also traded widely across Europe and the Mediterranean, and had well-developed religious beliefs expressed through the Druids. Many of the tribes, especially in the North, sustained opposition to the Roman occupation long after Boudicca's time. Scotland and Wales were never really subdued; Ireland was hardly touched. But there were, particularly in the South-East, cities and towns and country villas which did share in much of the Roman way of life

To induce a people, hitherto scattered, uncivilized and therefore prone to fight, to grow pleasurably inured to peace and ease, Agricola gave private encouragements and official assistance to the building of temples, public squares and private mansions. He praised the keen and scolded the slack, and competition to gain honour from him was as effective as compulsion. Furthermore, he trained the sons of the chiefs in the liberal arts and expressed a preference for British natural ability over the trained skill of the Gauls. The result was that in place of distaste for the Latin language came a passion to command it. In the same way, our national dress came into favour and the toga was everywhere to be seen. And so the Britons were gradually led on to the amenities that make vice agreeable – arcades, baths and sumptuous banquets. They spoke of such novelties as 'civilization', when really they were only a feature of enslavement.

Source 9 Translation of a passage from Tacitus (H. Mattingly, 'Agricola', in *Tacitus on Britain and Germany*. Penguin Classics, 1948, p. 72). This translation stays admirably close to Tacitus' original Latin

indicated by Tacitus: see for example Fishbourne Roman Palace, near Chichester.

Sources 10 and 10a are from early in the following, the second, century. This time it is written on stone. It is a memorial inscription for an officer in the Roman army who died while serving in the fortified garrison town of Deva (Chester), which was in the military zone and a port for troops sailing north or west. The legion XX Valeria Victrix, which had helped to defeat Boudicca, was stationed there.

Roman craftsmen made better lettering than anyone before them. So it cost quite a bit for a stone like this, and to save money and space, they used initial letters or abbreviations wherever they

could, just as we use 'HMS' or 'Co.'. Everyone would know what was meant. In this case, but not always, the words were separated by dots. The numbers were of course in Roman numerals: X for ten, V for five, and I for one.

The memorial in Sources 10 and 10a was dedicated, as was usual then, to the 'spirits of the departed'. Note that Caecilius Avitus came from what is now southern Spain (he probably found it rather cold at Deva, especially with his short Roman tunic covered with a warm cloak); that he was deputy officer to a centurion who commanded a 'century' (80 men, not 100, at that time); that he was only 34 when he died (in battle, or from illness?) and that he is shown with his sword, the staff showing his rank, and a writing tablet because part of his duties included clerical work. His heir paid for the stone, as people sometimes do today for their parents. Later, in about Alban's time in the early fourth century, this stone was actually used to repair the walls of Deva, where it was found two centuries ago and is now in the Grosvenor Museum in Chester.

Roman Britain was a favourite topic in primary schools long before the advent of the National Curriculum. Therefore there are many excellent resources, old and new, and much advice from publishers. Guide books to museums and local sites, postcards of Roman remains, and packs produced by LEAs amplify what is available. Visits to Roman sites, including Deva, figure in the programme of some primary schools. Much of the excellent work on Roman Britain now done within the National Curriculum is along well-established lines: maps of roads and cities and Hadrian's Wall, plans of amphitheatres, milecastles and villas, replicas of memorial stones, accounts of Boudicca's revolt and so on. These can be supplemented by using Sources 10 and 10a in the following ways:

SUGGESTED ACTIVITIES

- Rewrite in everyday language a part of what Tacitus wrote.
- Re-write what Tacitus said about Agricola's work, from the point of view of somebody who disapproved of Agricola.
- Work out, from his memorial, what Caecilius Avitus' heir thought important about him.
- From knowing where the memorial stone was found, consider whether we can say why it was broken at the knees.
- On an outline map of England and Wales, and using a map of Roman Britain in an atlas or in other books, mark Deva, and also some other important Roman centres such as Londinium, Eboracum (York), Verulamium (St Albans: see Source 12 on page 36), and Hadrian's Wall, and some of the most important roads. More places could be put in the part of the country round the school.

These activities are suitable for individual work for more able pupils and as a basis for discussion with younger children. (Saxon and Viking activities come later.)

For an event later in the Roman period in Britain (which lasted for nearly four hundred years) the martyrdom of St Alban (Source 12 on page 36) under one of the later emperors is included, and suggestions are made for work that could be based on that document. By that time the Saxons had begun to harry the shores of Britain. They gradually invaded and settled much of southern and eastern Britain, while the Britons survived and Roman rule decayed.

The extract about St Alban is one of the remaining five in this chapter. They are taken from the two best-known original sources for the other two topics in this chapter, the Venerable Bede's *Ecclesiastical History of the English Nation* and the compilation by generations of monks known as *The Anglo-Saxon Chronicle* (see Chapter 2, p. 17). Neither of these could have been written but for the conversion of the Anglo-Saxons to Christianity and of the consequent spread of literacy especially through the monastic foundations. But whereas Bede wrote in Latin, the *Chronicle*, begun at the behest of King Alfred in the ninth century, was written in Anglo-Saxon.

Source 10a   Memorial stone for Caecilius Avitus, transcribed and translated in Source 10

D	M		D(is) M(anibus)	To the spirits of the departed
CAECILIUS.AVIT			Caecilius Avit-	Caecilius Avitus
US.EMER.AVG			us Emer(ita) Aug(usta)	of Emerita Augusta
OPTIO.LEG.XX			Optio leg(ionis) XX	optio of the twentieth legion
VV.STP.XV.VIX			V(aleria) V(ictrix) st(i)p(endiorum) XV vix(it)	Valeria Victrix, with fifteen years' stipend, lived
AN.XXXIIII			an(nos) XXXIIII	for 34 years
H	F	C	h(aeres) f(aciendum) c(uravit)	his heir had this made

Source 10   Memorial stone for Caecilius Avitus, perhaps about the time of the Emperor Hadrian (117–138), who had the Wall built. Found during excavation of the walls of the fort of Deva, and now in the Grosvenor Museum, Chester. Reproduced by permission, and with the help of, the Grosvenor Museum

NOTES: Emerita Augusta, named after the Emperor Augustus, was in Hispania (Spain). It is now called Mérida: nearly the same name.

An Optio was second-in-command of a century (80 men, not 100).

'Victrix' means 'victorious', because of the victory over Boudicca. It is not clear who this Valerius was.

SOURCES FROM BEDE

The first of these extracts is in Source 11 and is about Bede himself. Written in about AD 731, it provides a simple and modest autobiography and declaration of faith. Although this one refers to a time later than the events in the next two, it seems appropriate to place it here, as an introduction to the historian of those events before his own lifetime. From the age of seven, Bede was educated at the monastery of Jarrow, near Newcastle-on-Tyne, and there he remained all his life as a scholar-monk, researching and writing his monumental *History* and other books of a similar sort.

The extract from Bede's writing in Source 12 is about an event which, as already mentioned, actually belongs to the Roman period. By the beginning of the fourth century AD, Christianity had spread quite widely in the Roman Empire (to be studied in Key Stage 3) but from time to time there was savage persecution by Emperors who required that worship should be directed towards themselves. During the last of these persecutions, early in the fourth century, a young soldier, Alban, who had become a Christian, was martyred outside the Roman city of Verulamium, on the site of the city in Hertfordshire which now bears

Thus much of the Ecclesiastical History of Britain, and more especially of the English nation, as far as I could learn either from the writings of the ancients, or of my own knowledge, has, with the help of God, been digested by me, Bede, the servant of God, and priest of the monastery of the blessed apostles, Peter and Paul, which is at Wearmouth and Jarrow; who being born in the territory of that same monastery, was given, at seven years of age, to be educated by the most reverend Abbat [sic] Benedict, and afterwards by Ceolfrid; and spending all the remaining time of my life in that monastery, I wholly applied myself to the study of Scripture, and amidst the observance of regular discipline, and the daily care of singing in the church, I always took delight in learning, teaching, and writing.

Source 11   Extract from Bede's *Ecclesiastical History of the English Nation*, written about AD 731, and translated into Victorian English (Everyman edition, 1939 reprint, J. M. Dent, p. 283)

his name. Alban suffered torture at the hands of a pagan high priest, and in spite of many favourable signs from heaven enabling him to work miracles, he met his death by the sword. We are told that the soldier first detailed to execute him was so impressed by Alban's faith that he refused to harm the prisoner and that he too became a Christian; whereupon another executioner was appointed and the first one suffered the same fate as Alban. Memory of this martyrdom was handed down by word of mouth and in some later records – the 'writings of the ancients' mentioned by Bede in Source 11 – so that Bede himself was able to write this passage, four centuries later.

'I am called Alban by my parents', replied he; 'and I worship and adore the true and living God, who created all things'.

When the judge perceived that he was not to be overcome by tortures, or withdrawn from the exercise

of the Christian religion, he ordered him to be put to death.

On the top of this hill, St. Alban prayed that God would give him water, and immediately a living spring broke out before his feet. . . . Here . . . the head of our most courageous martyr was struck off, and here he received the crown of life, which God has promised to those who love Him.

Source 12   Extracts from Bede's *Ecclesiastical History of the English Nation*, written early in the eighth century AD, and translated into Victorian English (Everyman edition, 1939 reprint, J. M. Dent, pp. 12 and 13)

The remaining extract from Bede in Source 13 and is about another event of central importance to an 'ecclesiastical history', which took place nearly three centuries later. It is important to emphasise the great spans of time within this chapter. Christianity had taken root rather shakily in the last phase of Roman Britain, and had spread to Ireland and Scotland; but the Anglo-Saxons came as pagans and Christianity almost disappeared from England. Later it was reintroduced, first as 'Celtic' Christianity from Ireland and Scotland, and later, with the blessing of Pope Gregory the Great, from Rome. He sent the mission everybody remembers ('not Angles, but angels') headed by Augustine, which introduced 'Roman' Christianity to Britain again. Augustine had heard of the cruelty of the Angles, Saxons and Jutes, and at first he was reluctant to go to Angle-land, but Gregory persuaded him to set forth.

His colourful procession met the pagan King of (Jutish) Kent, Ethelbert, in the open air for safety, near his capital Canterbury. Ethelbert, whose Queen, Bertha, had already become a Christian, was so impressed that he allowed Augustine's monks to stay and preach with Canterbury as their centre. (The Archbishopric, or See, of Canterbury dates from this time.) Read half the source first, to emphasise visually the approach of Augustine's procession of monks.

Some days after, the king [Ethelbert] came into the island [Thanet], and sitting in the open air, ordered Augustine and his companions to be brought into his presence. For he had taken precaution that they should not come to him in any house, lest, according to an ancient superstition, if they practised any magical arts, they might impose upon him, and so get the better of him. But they came furnished with the Divine, not with magic virtue, bearing a silver cross for their banner, and the image of our Lord and Saviour painted on a board; and singing the litany, they offered up their prayers to the Lord for the eternal salvation both of themselves and of those to whom they were come.

When he had sat down, pursuant to [following] the king's commands, and preached to him and his attendants there present, the word of life, the king answered thus: – Your words and promises are very fair, but as they are new to us, and of uncertain import, I cannot approve of them so far as to forsake that which I have so long followed with the whole English nation. But because you are come from far into my kingdom, and, as I conceive, are desirous to

impart to us those things which you believe to be true, and most beneficial, we will not molest you, but give you favourable entertainment, and take care to supply you with your necessary sustenance; nor do we forbid you to preach and gain as many as you can to your religion. Accordingly he permitted them to reside in the city of Canterbury, which was the metropolis of all his dominions, and, pursuant to his promise, besides allowing them sustenance, did not refuse them liberty to preach.

Source 13   Extract from Bede's *Ecclesiastical History of the English Nation*, AD 597, written early in the eighth century AD, and translated into Victorian English (Everyman edition, 1939 reprint, J. M. Dent, pp. 35–6)

Roman missionaries benefited from this royal support in which Bertha took an active part, and they spread the gospel into other Anglo-Saxon kingdoms. But it was not until 625, after Augustine's death, that one of his monks, Paulinus, went to Northumbria to explain the Roman form of Christianity in a land where the Celtic form was established. Only in 664, at the Synod of Whitby, were the two forms brought together, with more emphasis being laid on Roman customs, such as when Easter should be celebrated.

VIKING INVASIONS

The next two extracts in this chapter (Sources 14 and 15) are from the *Anglo-Saxon Chronicle*, and both are about the Viking invasions and the Saxon resistance to them. So they remind us how, in time, the Anglo-Saxons and the Vikings overlap: there is no time at which one ended and the other began. At first the marauding Danes came in powerful sea-going warships, but after a while they built up a fighting force on land, which the *Chronicle* writers always referred to simply as 'the army'. This force ravaged and plundered the countryside, and especially the comparatively rich

but defenceless monasteries, with a view to establishing Danish settlements. As pagans, they had no particular veneration for abbots or monks.

In the first of these extracts from the *Chronicle*, King Edmund of East Anglia tried to resist 'the army', and paid for his efforts with his life.

AD 870. This year the army rode over Mercia into East-Anglia, and there fixed their winter-quarters at Thetford. And in the winter King Edmund fought with them; but the Danes gained the victory, and slew the king; whereupon they overran all that land,

*and destroyed all the monasteries to which they came.
The names of the leaders who slew the king were
Hingwar and Hubba. At the same time came they to
Medhamsted, burning and breaking, and slaying
abbot and monks, and all that they there found. They
made such havoc there, that a monastery, which was
before full rich, was now reduced to nothing.*

Source 14 Extract from *The Anglo-Saxon Chronicle,*
translated by Rev. James Ingram (version published in
Everyman series, J. M. Dent, reprinted 1938, p. 64).
King Edmund of East Anglia was tied to a tree, pierced
with arrows and then had his head cut off

The extract in Source 14 chosen because it
presents, in simple, stark, terms, the realities of
the invasion. The Danes attacked at first up the
wide estuaries of the east coast of England, but
subsequently they went almost everywhere.
Meanwhile the Norsemen (Norwegians) raided
Scotland and Ireland and established settlements
there.

But the Danes did not have it all their own way.
Their 'army' was sometimes mauled. Some of
their effort was diverted into attacks on
Normandy, whose name shows that it was
conquered by the Norse-men. In Alfred the Great,
King of Wessex from 871 to 900, they met an
opponent who could fight them on equal terms.
In the words of one authority, R. H. Hodgkin, 'he
must be the centre of any picture of Saxon times',

and he was the only leader in British history to be
called 'the Great', except for the later Dane,
Canute. The final extract (Source 15) shows one
example of what he did.

*This same year [897] the plunderers in East-Anglia
and Northumbria greatly harassed the land of the
West-Saxons by piracies on the southern coast, but
most of all by the esks [Danish warships] which they
built many years before. The King Alfred gave orders
for building long ships against the esks, which were
full-nigh twice as long as the others. Some had sixty
oars, some more; and they were both swifter and
steadier, and also higher than the others. They were
not shaped either after the Frisian or the Danish
model, but so as he himself thought that they might be
most serviceable.*

Source 15 Extract from *The Anglo-Saxon Chronicle,*
translated by Rev. James Ingram (version published in
Everyman series, J. M. Dent, reprinted 1938, p. 75)

Alfred realised that ships of superior design
were needed by Wessex if the Danes were to be
defeated. This may be regarded as the beginning
of the British naval tradition. Later, after he had
fought off the Danes, he made peace with their
leader Guthrum (at Wedmore in 878), allowing
him control over the North and East of England
while he kept the rest, the Kingdom of Wessex.
(Wessex eventually became the basis of the
Kingdom of England.)

THE VIKINGS

Sources 16 and 17 convey something more about
the Vikings themselves, especially the Norsemen.
The first is from a collection of sagas brought
together in the thirteenth century by a remarkable
Icelander, Snorri Sturluson. It tells how, in his old
age, King Harald Fine-Hair of Norway had made
his favourite son, Eric Blood-Axe, his regent. After
Harald died, Eric seized his father's throne and

killed two other brothers, but the people of
Norway did not like him. Then another brother,
Hakon, gradually won the support of the people.
Source 16 takes up the tale at that point.

*As he saw himself not nearly strong enough to oppose
Hakon, he [King Eric] sailed out to the West with
such men as would follow him. He first sailed to*

Orkney, and took many people with him from that country; and then went south towards England, plundering in Scotland, and in the north parts of England, wherever he could land. Athelstan, the king of England, sent a message to Eric, offering him dominions under him in England; saying that King Harald his father was a good friend of King Athelstan, and therefore he would do kindly towards his son. Messengers passed between the two kings; and it came to an agreement that King Eric should take Northumberland [Northumbria] as a fief from King Athelstan, and this land he should defend against the Danes or other vikings. Eric accepted this offer, and was baptised, together with his wife and children, and all the people who followed him. Northumberland is called a fifth part of England. Eric had his residence at York, where Lodbrok's sons, it is said, had formerly been, and Northumberland was principally inhabited by Northmen, after Lodbrok's sons had taken the country. Danes and Northmen often plundered there, when the power of the land was out of their hands. Many names of places in the country are Norwegian; as Grimsby . . .

Source 16 Extract from Snorri Sturluson (*Heimskringla*, Part Two, *Sagas of the Norse Kings*, London: Everyman's Library, 1930, revised 1951, pp. 85–6). Lodbrok was a Dane who had been with 'the army' (see Source 14)

It shows how a defeated king would try his fortune at sea, as Vikings did. It also shows how violent the times were. Note that:

- Athelstan, King of Wessex, grandson of Alfred the Great, was well respected by these Norwegian kings. Hakon had been brought up in Athelstan's court.
- York (Jorvik, the former Roman Eboracum) had by now become a great centre of Viking peacetime civilisation. Evidence for this is displayed in the Jorvik Museum.

Of course these Viking leaders depended on the support of men to whom the sea was home and the source of plunder, and Source 17 captures their spirit, though in fact this poet was a Saxon, trying to understand the mind of the raiders.

To finish off the story as Storri Sturluson told it: Eric Blood-Axe did not really settle in Northumbria. He went on Viking expeditions every summer. After Athelstan died, his successor as King of Wessex had Eric killed and his family driven out. So they went raiding around the British seas. In the end they went to Denmark and then to Norway where they killed Hakon. Remember that the Norsemen from Norway and the Danes were often at war with each other, though, for a short time in the new millennium, Denmark, England and Norway were all under one king, Canute (Knut) the Great.

SUGGESTED ACTIVITIES

Like Tacitus' account, but in a less sophisticated style, sources 11 to 16 are narrative accounts of events showing bias and interpretation in the way they are told. Their first use in school would be for the teacher to read parts aloud and to adapt them for story-telling. The longest (Source 13), about Augustine, could be divided into two: the missionaries' arrival, and Ethelbert's reception; each could be used separately. This story-telling could lead to class discussions:

- What bias is shown?
- What happened to Alban and why do you think Christians were treated like this?
- Did monks like Bede do anything else than write? How could they react when they were attacked, for example by Vikings?

•Who would die for what belief now, as Alban did then?

•Why did Vikings leave Norway to roam the seas?

With older juniors, each extract could be reproduced for children to use in pairs, and the teacher could draw up a question sheet about the extract:

- Comparisons could be made between how the seven year-old Bede wrote with how the children themselves are now learning to write. They should think about: quill pens; parchment; scriptorium (a writing room in a monastery)
- Other comparisons could be made between what Bede wrote about and what the members of the class might write about today
- The more colourful episodes such as Alban's execution and Ethelbert's welcome to Augustine, give scope for role-playing in groups.

- Using a map of the British Isles (with which children at Key Stage 2 are becoming familiar), find the route followed by Eric when he left Norway.
- A list could be made of local Danish or Norwegian place-names, the ones that end in -by, -thorpe, -toft and often -kirk. Some of them also include personal names. Of course these names are mostly, but not only, found in the parts where the Danes and Norsemen settled. Local histories often include information about place-names. They (and much else) can be found in the *Concise Oxford Dictionary of English Place Names*, compiled by Eilert Ekwall.
- Perhaps a group song could be composed as though it had been made up by the crew of one of Alfred's new ships, or by a Viking going to sea with Eric. You may like to compare Source 17 with John Masefield's 'Sea Fever': John Ireland made it into a song. A sea song usually has verses and a chorus, and sometimes has actions to go with the words and music.

I can sing	*my own true story*
Tell of my travels	*how I have oft suffered*
Times of hardship	*in days of toil*
Bitter cares	*have I often harboured,*
And often learned	*how troubled a home*
Is a ship in a storm,	*when I took my turn*
At the arduous night-watch	*at the vessel's prow*
As it beat past cliffs.	*Oft were my feet*
Fettered by frost	*in frozen bonds,*
Tortured by cold,	*while searing anguish*
Clutched at my heart	*and longing rent*
My sea-weary mind . . .	
	. . . Yet now once more
	to try again
My heart's blood stirs me	*the salt waves' play;*
The towering seas,	*always urge me*
My heart's desires	*to visit the lands*
To go on the journey	*far over the sea . . .*
Of foreign peoples	

Source 17 Extract showing the Viking spirit, from the Anglo-Saxon poem *The Seafarer* (from the *Exeter Book*, quoted in Magnus Magnusson, *Vikings*, BBC, published by the Bodley Head, 1980, pp. 23–4)

For the Saxon period, it is worthwhile to find and use a copy of a translation of the *Anglo-Saxon Chronicle* itself. Although it is not without bias (why?), it has local references to almost every part of the country, and it would be useful to build some activities round the references to a school's own area, for local history is not just recent history. Other kinds of written work could be based on material from other sources such as the poetry which belonged to the culture, for example *The Song of Beowulf* or archaeological finds such as the Sutton Hoo Ship Burial. Or

there could be a closer study of the different aspects of King Alfred's reign and the culture of the time: quite a lot is known about this. If the Vikings are the focus of concentration, more could be found out about how they lived at home, and about where else they 'colonised': Normandy, Sicily, Russia (remember that Snorri Sturluson was an Icelander). For the extracts included in this chapter are intended only to provide a part of the resources available to teachers, one which is not always so easily accessible but which can bring to life the people of an age in a unique way.

FIVE

Life in Tudor times

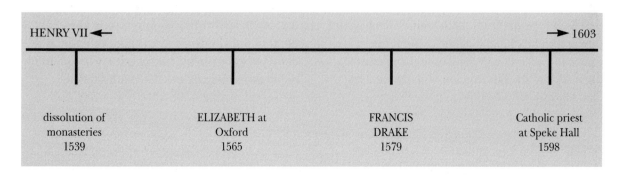

HENRY VII ←			→ 1603
dissolution of monasteries 1539	ELIZABETH at Oxford 1565	FRANCIS DRAKE 1579	Catholic priest at Speke Hall 1598

Written sources are plentiful for the Tudor period, when compared with the subject-matter of Chapter 4, and transcriptions make it easier to read sixteenth-century handwriting which is otherwise rather baffling. Most Record Offices (city, county or diocesan) have an Archivist able to transcribe a difficult hand for a small charge (see Robert Brerewood's inventory in Source 48 on page 87). Stuart documents, which some schools had used, may be used where appropriate in local history (see Chapter 8) or even at Key Stage 1 if they are well illustrated, like the one on this book's cover.

Examples of topics not indicated in the 1995 Order include Mary Stuart, Parliamentary and foreign affairs. Some teachers may regret this. That is understandable, especially if a school has been accustomed to looking at these, and in particular at Mary of Scotland. Her presence was very important to Elizabeth I and her statesmen, and her life story is colourful, dramatic and tragic. In any case the Order requires that attention should be paid where relevant to Scotland, Wales and Ireland. Of course, part of Mary's life when she was imprisoned in Bolton Castle, Yorkshire, could be chosen in local history – 'a short period linked to national events' – and similarly in other localities directly associated with her. These omitted topics are not formally forbidden in 'Life in Tudor Times' itself! But in practice even Mary is likely to be crowded out by the ones that have to be included. The sources considered in this chapter illustrate some of those.

THE DISSOLUTION OF THE MONASTERIES

Henry VIII's dissolution of the monasteries (1536–39) is one of those; a central feature of the English Reformation during the course of which Henry replaced the Pope as 'Supreme Head' of the Church of England. The extract in Source 18 is an example of how Thomas Cromwell, Henry's Lord Chancellor, sent Commissioners (visitors) round monasteries to find evidence to justify closing them and confiscating their wealth. On 22 September 1539 Richard Pollard, Thomas Moyle and Richard Langton visited the wealthy abbey of Glastonbury, and Source 18 is part of their report.

And so with as fair words as we could, we have conveyed him [the abbot] from hence into the tower, being but a very weak man and sickly. And as yet we have neither discharged servant nor monk; but now the abbot being gone, we will, with as much celerity as we may, proceed to the despatching of them . . . This is also to advertise [inform] your lordship, that we have found a fair chalice [communion wine cup] of gold, and divers other parcels of plate [silver or gold table ware], which the abbot had hid secretly from all such commissioners as have been there in times past; and as yet he knoweth not that we have found the same. It may please your lordship to advertise us of the king's pleasure by this bearer, to whom we shall deliver the custody and keeping of the house, with such stuff as we intend to leave there convenient to the king's use. We assure your lordship it is the goodliest house of that sort that we ever have seen. We would that your lordship did know it as we do; then we doubt not but your lordship would judge it a house meet for the king's majesty and for no man else: which is to our great comfort; and we trust verily that there shall never come any double hood [cowl of a Benedictine monk] within that house again.

Source 18 Extract from report to Thomas Cromwell by Commissioners, on a visitation to Glastonbury Abbey, 1539 (quoted in C. R. N. Routh, *They Saw it Happen, 1485–1688*. Oxford: Basil Blackwell, 1956, pp. 29–30)

These men were biased from the outset against the abbot and monks; that is why they were Commissioners. In their letter to Cromwell they wrote of their rapid transfer of the abbot to the Tower of London and of the great wealth awaiting the king. They do not describe the running of the monastery as corrupt, but they do recognise that its wealth was so great as to be fit only for Henry. It is likely that the abbot was executed and the monks pensioned off, or allowed to wander the roads as pauper 'vagrants'. To be fair to Henry, some of the monasteries really were corrupt, with few monks living in them.

Monastic lands, having been taken over for the king, were often given to his favourites. The buildings were not demolished. Some were incorporated into cathedrals, as in the case of St Werburgh's Abbey in Chester which became the centre of a new diocese. Others eventually became ruins through lack of use, though many of them, including Glastonbury, were so well built 'to the greater glory of God' that their remains still indicate how large and impressive they once were. Children are probably aware of local examples and can be encouraged to visit them with their families. Ideally there could be a class visit, if the time, cost and organisation can be justified. (It may be more appropriate to carry out a visit at Key Stage 3 when the medieval world is being studied.)

QUEEN ELIZABETH I AT OXFORD

Henry VIII's daughter Elizabeth I extended her control over the nobility (as her grandfather Henry VII had done) and made herself popular with her people by 'progressing' round the country, especially its southern parts. As an intellectual queen, in an age when scholarship was in fashion, she liked showing off her knowledge of Latin (and Greek) whenever she visited the only two English universities, Oxford

and Cambridge. (Gresham College, founded in London in her reign, never actually became a university: Scotland already had three; Ireland had its first at this time.) When she visited Oxford, she stayed in Christ Church with her entourage of courtiers and servants. This college had been founded by Cardinal Wolsey, Henry VIII's chief minister before Thomas Cromwell. The Queen's visit cost the College a pretty penny (she always charged her expenses to her hosts) and sometimes this caused real hardship and resentment although probably not at well-endowed Christ Church. There she enjoyed in 1565 a performance of *Palamon and Arcite*, written specially for her visit by Richard Edwardes, a senior member of the College. The play itself has not survived, but we hope it was a comedy: we learn from an author living early in the seventeenth century that she 'laughed heartily thereat, and gave the author great thanks for his pains'. Dr Reynolds, of Corpus Christi College, next door to Christ Church, as a younger man played the part of a woman in this play. Source 19 is a description of the occasion by a traveller through England in her reign. Children should be encouraged to read the Elizabethan spelling, which is easily understood. They can then be asked to rewrite the passage in today's English

'Palamon and Arcite'

1565. The Queene of England beginneth hir progress, & vpon the 31 of August coming to Oxford, where she visiteth eche college after other, & making an oration vnto them in Latine, as she had done in Cambridge two yeres passed, to the gret comfort of all soche as are, or had bene, students there. During her being there also the Academicall exercises [oral examination of students] were holden as in their vsuall termes. Diuerse Commedies & plaies also were set forthe by the studentes of Christes Church, where her Majestie lodged; but of all the rest, onely that of 'Arcite and Palamon' had a tragicall successe; for, by the falle of a walle & wooden gallery that leadeth from the staires vnfinished to the hall, diuers persons were sore hurt, & 3 men killed out right, which came to behold the pastimes.

Source 19   Extract about one of Elizabeth I's 'progresses', from William Harrison's *Chronologie* (reproduced in the Appendix to Lothrop Withington (ed), *Elizabethan England*, with introduction by F. J. Furnivall, The Scott Library, Walter Scott Ltd, c.1876)

SIR FRANCIS DRAKE

Source 20 represents the importance of overseas adventure to Elizabethan England. The Spanish king, Philip II, had been married to Elizabeth's sister, Queen Mary Tudor, before Elizabeth succeeded her. At one time he had designs on Elizabeth herself. Philip owned lands rich in precious metals in South and Central America – the 'New World' (new, that is, to Europeans). The English 'buccaneers', really pirates, preyed on Spanish ships laden with gold and silver from these new colonies. Francis Drake (see Chapter 9, p. 92), from one of the families which had recently benefited from the sale of monastic lands, stands out as one of the most important individual seaman (see 1995 Order), though others played their part, notably John Hawkins

and Sir Richard Grenville. After carrying out some piratical expeditions along the 'Spanish Main', now the Atlantic coast from Costa Rica to Venezuela, he sailed round the world in 1577–80. Our source was written by a Spanish admiral who had been captured with his ship by Drake during that epic voyage but was subsequently released. In Source 20 he is telling the Spanish Viceroy, Philip's representative in the Spanish colonies, about Drake's capabilities as a seaman and a leader. The admiral noted Drake's expensive tastes in food and in eating utensils. Drake would naturally invite a captured admiral to eat with him at his Captain's table, such was the strict etiquette across Europe at that time.

The General of the English is a nephew of Juan Aquines [John Hawkins] and is the same man who five years ago took the port of Nombre de Dios. He is called Francisco Drac and may be a man of thirty-five years of age, very small in stature, with a red beard, and one of the best sailors there is at sea, not only as an observer of latitude but as a commander of his ship. He has a galleon of about four hundred tons, a finished sailer [well-tried ship], and a hundred men, all fit and of a proper age for war, and all as well disciplined as the old Italian soldiers; particularly, every one takes great care to have his harquebus [portable gun on a tripod] clean . . . He is served with much plate with his arms on it, which has the borders and the decorations gilded. He carries with him all the presents [sweetmeats] and scented water possible, much of which he said had been given to him by the Queen.

When he returned from his 'circumnavigation', Francis Drake was knighted by Queen Elizabeth on his 'home ground', Plymouth Hoe. You can see his statue there today. His ship, the Golden Hind, brought home much wealth for the Queen as well as for himself. In the next few years he carried out more expeditions against Spain, and played a major part in defeating Philip's famous Armada in 1588, as can be found in any standard book about Elizabeth's reign. But his last venture in the 'New World' was less successful and he died of a fever in what is now Panama, in 1586.

Source 20 Extract from a letter from Francisco de Zárate to Viceroy Martin Enriques, in 1579, after he had been released by Drake following capture of his ship (though there was not much booty on board). (Translated into modern English in Henry R. Wagner, *Sir Francis Drake's Voyage Around the World: its Aims and Achievements.* San Francisco: John Howell, 1926, pp. 375–6.) Nombre de Dios ('Name of God') was a Spanish town on the Atlantic coast of what is now Panama: Drake eventually died on board ship there. Soldiers from Northern Italy were renowned at that time for their military prowess, and were often hired as mercenaries

CATHOLIC PRIESTS IN HIDING

The last extract, about religious life at the end of the sixteenth century, links with the first. The dissolution of the monasteries had shown that Henry VIII was no longer obedient to the Pope (this was partly due to the problems about having a male heir) but he still considered himself a Catholic.

Before the end of Elizabeth I's reign there were signs that she definitely favoured the new Protestants. By 1598, after the Armada (the climax of her wars with Philip II), she taxed Catholics heavily for not attending the parish church, which now meant the Church of England. This tax was imposed under the *Recusancy Laws* (a *recusant* is someone who refuses to attend church as required) and for harbouring Roman Catholic priests in their houses .The Norris family of Speke Hall, near Liverpool, were rightly suspected of being Catholics: the north-west of England was the centre of Roman Catholic under-cover opposition to the Queen. In fact John Gerard, one of the most famous Catholic priests trained on the continent to serve in England, was born and bred in Lancashire. Edward Norris, a wealthy 'gentleman' with many Catholic contacts, kept two priests at Speke Hall; the Norris family had made many 'priest-holes' in unlikely places.

In Source 21, written three years after Drake's death, John Bird, a Catholic 'informer' or traitor, tells Robert Cecil, now the Queen's chief minister, that 'little Sir Richard', a priest unrelated to the Norris family, was hiding in Speke Hall. When royal 'visitors' came to the Hall, 'Little Sir Richard' took on the role of a servant waiting at table. Edward had nine children and John Bird believes that they were all brought up as good Catholics.

In Lancastershire at a place called the Speake, dwelleth one Edward Norris an esquiour of vC li* in livel'hood whoe being a knowne Recusant harboreth two priests: of whome, the one is called Little Sir Richard, or Sir Richard Norris, and the other Sir Peter, for the most parte lodged in a Chamber over the parlor, and at what tymes strangers visite the howse, the said Sir Richard waiteth at the Table as a servingman in a liverie coate and cognisaunce [coat of arms and badge], his children [Edward's] as they have ben borne, educated, and married are said to be christened, married & buried with masses & Romish Ceremonies . . .

Source 21 Extract from a letter written to Mr Secretary Cecil by an informer, 1598, about a priest in hiding, Richard Norris, at Speke Hall near Liverpool (Hatfield House, Cecil Papers, 58/103). Reproduced by permission of the Marquess of Salisbury
* An 'esquiour of vC li in livel'hood' means 'A squire worth £500 a year' [vC = 5 × 100; li(bra) = pound. The Roman 'D', for 500, must not have been in use by this informer.

SUGGESTED ACTIVITIES

These four sources represent the reigns of the two most prominent Tudor monarchs, Henry VIII and Elizabeth I. They are concerned however with the more wealthy sectors of Tudor England. Religion was closely connected with politics and society in the sixteenth (and seventeenth) century and therefore figures prominently in the sources. These should be explained by the teacher with the help of this chapter and of the notes given after each extract. It would be helpful to provide one copy of the sources themselves for each pair of children so that if the teacher reads them aloud, the children can follow. Class discussion can easily be introduced by the teacher with such questions as:

- Were the visitors to Glastonbury Abbey more interested in the poor conditions in the Abbey or in its wealth?
- What sort of men were seamen on Drake's ship *The Golden Hind*?
- Would you rather have been Edward Norris or 'little Sir Richard'?
- Why?

A second kind of activity might be to prepare several questions for each extract on an A4 sheet, for the children to work on in pairs. A selection of their answers could then be read out and

discussed at the end of the session. It would be better to undertake this activity when all the sources have been studied.

Thirdly, if the teacher wanted to set an individual task covering two sessions, the children could each try to write an imaginative account from a point of view different from that of the writer. Non-fiction texts could be used to provide children with additional information. Here are some ideas:

- A monk at Glastonbury defends his monastery in a letter to Thomas Cromwell
- A student at Christ Church writes home describing Queen Elizabeth's visit to his college
- A seaman sailing with Drake tells his 'girl friend', when he returns to port, about the capture and release of the Spanish admiral
- Edward Norris tells his son William about the visit of the Queen's spies to find the two priests, and chuckles about how they were hidden

These suggestions show that, as already indicated, 'Life in Tudor Times' is best taught to older juniors, Years 5 and 6. But younger children may be able to understand the teacher's explanation of the source material, and could be encouraged to form groups for the four topics to discuss how they could role-play the various episodes, an experience which could also of course benefit the older children. Good examples would be: a meal at Drake's Captain's Table, with the Spanish admiral as an unwilling guest; or a banquet at Speke Hall with 'little Sir Richard' waiting at table on the Queen's spies. Whichever way this period is handled with any age-group, it would be helpful to bring it to a climax by preparing and mounting, and being ready to explain, a class exhibition about one or more of the topics in the context of a Tudor time chart – about the age in general.

In any treatment of 'Life in Tudor Times', attention should also be paid to social history, the 'ways of life in town and country' of the English National Curriculum suggestions. In sixteenth century writings, attention was gradually being paid nationally to such matters, impelled by social changes which were taking place, but extracts from writers such as Sir Thomas More are not generally suitable for young children because they deal with these issues on too broad a plane. However, there is a place for using local sources, where they are available, for close-up studies. Parish records, throwing light on questions such as road maintenance and poor relief, may be accessible for Elizabethan times, but rarely before.

It is rather more promising to look for probate inventories (see Sources 48 and 49 in Chapter 8), which can be more readily discovered in local archives. References to localities may be found in contemporary sources such as Leland's *Itineray* and Camden's *Britannia.* But it may be difficult to justify pursuing written sources of these kinds unless a local study from Tudor times is chosen for more substantial study (see Chapter 8). For such reasons, we have not included examples of this kind of material in this chapter. These aspects of Tudor social history are better handled at Key Stage 2 from more general books designed for this purpose, rather than from contemporary sources, which some children may encounter later.

With both younger and older juniors, it is more productive for a teacher first to explain the sources, and then to organise activities. Children can then look for other, more informative, books in the school or in public libraries, and perhaps also illustrative material from museums and art galleries, and perhaps pursue other, related, interests. The National Gallery, the National Portrait Gallery and the Walker Art Gallery in Liverpool are examples of the more important national sources; but there are many excellent local sources, and many well-equipped Education Officers to advise, if questions are carefully thought out before they are asked. The scope for a rich treatment of 'Life in Tudor Times' is evident, and can be very rewarding for teachers and children alike.

Victorian Britain

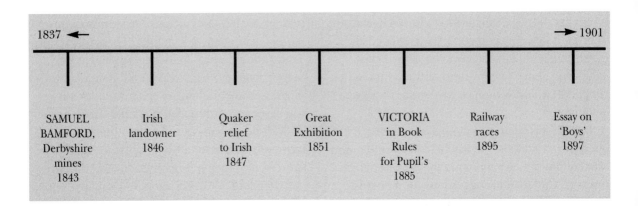

1837 ←						→ 1901
SAMUEL BAMFORD, Derbyshire mines 1843	Irish landowner 1846	Quaker relief to Irish 1847	Great Exhibition 1851	VICTORIA in Book Rules for Pupil's 1885	Railway races 1895	Essay on 'Boys' 1897

This chapter is clearly about *Victorian* Britain, from the Queen's accession in 1837, and about Victorian *Britain*, not just England, though our sources reflect the emphasis on England in the English National Curriculum. At the same time it is important to remember that Victoria's 'sixty glorious years' (actually 64) were a period of immense social *change*, and that this should be emphasised in any work on Victorian Britain. Talk about 'the Victorians' should not be encouraged.

Victorian Britain has been so well resourced that it is quite difficult to add written sources usefully to what is already available. But some less readily accessible ones have been chosen here, to show something of 'changes in industry and transport' and 'the lives of people at different levels of society in town and country', as the 1995 English Order for History indicates.

SAMUEL BAMFORD AND FACTORY LIFE

Unlike many sources illuminating factory life in the *early* Victorian period, Samuel Bamford, who started life as a young pre-Victorian participant in the 'domestic system', gives a rather favourable view of the living conditions of employees in one South Lancashire factory. Writing in 1844 about his visit to the mill of 'M.C.' at High Crompton,

near Rochdale, he noticed that weavers in charge of four looms were helped by 'tenters' (see the note at the end of Source 22). Actually Bamford was a well-known Radical, and almost apologised for not painting conditions in this mill as worse than they actually were!

Mr. C. employed sixty-seven power-loom weavers of cords and velveteens. The weavers generally superintended two looms each, several had three looms, and one or two had four looms, the latter being assisted tenters [assistants who 'tended' the looms], whom they had to pay. A weaver of average ability, would earn, on two looms, from ten to twelve shillings per week; one with three looms, would get from thirteen to fourteen shillings; and one with four looms, would earn as much as fifteen shillings a week clear. A number of the hands lived in houses belonging to Mr. C., for which they paid from one shilling and sixpence, to two shillings and nine-pence per week, and their rent was settled every pay day.*

I made excuses to enter some of the houses, and found them uniformly neat and clean, one tenement was beautifully clean; the walls were as white as lime could make them; the good housewife, who was up to the elbows in suds, gave me liberty to see her chambers [bedrooms], and I found the walls and the beds on a par with the house below; they were almost spotless, and the air was as untainted as the wind. This was one of a row of houses; several others which I entered were almost in as good condition; they had generally flowers and green shrubs in the windows, and before the doors were small gardens with flowers and a few pot herbs. The tenements consisted of a front room, a kitchen, and two chambers; and the front rooms were furnished with handsome fire-grates, ovens, and boilers, all as well burnished as black lead, a good brush, and a willing hand could make them. The rent of those dwellings was two shillings and nine-pence per week, clear of all rates.

Source 22 Extract from Samuel Bamford, *Walks in South Lancashire and on its Borders*, written in the early 1840s (edition with introduction by J. B. Marshall. London: Harvester Press, 1972, pp. 32–3). This extract is about High Crompton, a village near Rochdale

*An alternative interpretation of 'assisted tenters' could be 'assisted by tenters', that is, by people who stretched the finished cloth 'on tenterhooks'.

After the teacher has read out the first part of this source up to 'pay day', the children in pairs could be set the problem of suggesting how the workers spent their wages: those earning 10/-, and 13/-, and 15/-. Some of them had to pay 2/9d per week rent for a cottage. (Remember that women and children earned too.) After discussing this problem in class for fifteen minutes or so, a teacher could read out the second part of the extract, and again children in pairs could make what might have been a plan of a typical workers' cottage and put in pieces of furniture and other essentials mentioned in the written sources. This could lead to quite searching questions:

- How was life in those cottages different from life today?
- How much money did the poorest workers have left after they had paid their rent?

Other mills were, as already mentioned, quite different from High Crompton. Millowners sometimes exploited the children whom they had accepted as indentured apprentices by illegally working them well outside the permitted hours (these mills were now regulated by law) and by making them save production time by oiling and cleaning machinery while it was running, sometimes with tragic results. On the other hand, there were a few owners who established 'model' mills and themselves had cottages built and doctors provided for their employees. Such were Samuel Greg of Quarry Bank Mill, Styal, and Titus Salt, who founded the mill and village of Saltaire.

CHILDREN IN THE COAL MINES

It was not only in cotton mills that conditions of work, including children's work, seem horrifying

to a modern reader. The plight of chimney-sweeps at that time will be well-known to readers of Charles Kingsley's *Water Babies*. Perhaps less familiar is the condition of children of both sexes in the coal mines on which, by now, the bulk of industry depended for power. Very young children were employed just because they could squeeze into spaces too narrow for adults, while their paltry wages augmented the meagre family budgets. But their conditions of work were so atrocious, and their hours of work so long, that Parliamentary commissions were established to look into them. In 1842 a Mines Act was passed, forbidding the employment in the mines of women or girls or of boys under ten, and setting up inspectors to see that this law was enforced.

Source 23 refers to coal mines in Derbyshire and Nottinghamshire. It is part of a report, prepared in 1843, just after the Mines Act and before Bamford wrote about High Crompton. It shows how harsh conditions still were, and that the law was apparently being broken: Thomas Straw was only seven. But desperate parents sometimes connived in law-breaking for the sake of children's wage packets.

In this district, the hours of work are commonly 14, and are sometimes extended to 16 out of 14 [from 14 to 16], and the mines in general are most imperfectly drained and ventilated . . .

Thomas Straw, aged seven, Ilkiston [now spelled Ilkeston]: They wouldn't let him sleep in the pit or stand still; he feels very tired when he comes out; gets his tea and goes to bed. John Hawkins, aged eight, Underwood; Is tired and glad to get home; never wants to play. Robert Blount, aged ten, Eastwood; He is always too tired to play, and is glad to get to bed; his back and legs ache; he had rather drive plough [sic] or go to school than work in a pit. John Bostock, aged seventeen, Babbington; Has often been made to work until he was so tired as to lie down on his road home until twelve o'clock, when his mother has come and led him home – has done so many times when he first went to the pits; he has sometimes been so fatigued that he could not eat his dinner, but has been beaten and made to work until night; he never thought of play, was always too anxious to get to bed.

Source 23 Extract about parts of Derbyshire and Nottinghamshire from *Report on the Physical and Moral Condition of the Children and Young Persons engaged in Mines and Manufactures*, London, 1843 (reproduced in T. Charles-Edwards and Brian Richardson, *They Saw it Happen, 1689–1897*. Oxford: Basel Blackwell, 1958, p. 242). The place-names are all in mining areas

SUGGESTED ACTIVITIES

Sources 22 and 23, about factories and mines, could be used by the teacher as source material about both.

- Class discussions, teacher-led, could compare the two, showing how easy it is to write with bias.
- It would be useful also to compare them with Bamford's much earlier experience, working with his aunt on a spinning wheel (p. 80) in the 'domestic' textile industry. Was boredom preferable to acute tiredness?
- After this close comparison, children could work in pairs to compare their own daily time-tables with those of Thomas Straw, John

Hawkins or Robert Blount.
- This might lead in turn to individual written comparisons between their life and that of one of the boys working in a mine in the 1840s.
- The girls too might make similar comparisons, remembering that by 1843 the Derbyshire girls would not have been allowed down the pits, though the work of the lasses noted by Bamford at High Crompton was quite legal.

Harsh conditions were also found in other industries until, one by one, they were subject to stricter regulations, including some provision of schooling, as Victoria's reign passed. But, as in the mines, these laws were often broken and children were found asleep in their school hours because their employers still made them work so long, as contemporary documents show. One well-known point of view, based on experience in Manchester, is given by Friedrich Engels in his *Condition of the Working Class in England in 1844*, one of the Marxist classics. Other contemporary sources include inspectors' reports, first on textile mills and then on other industries, and the proceedings of the Parliamentary committees who interviewed people engaged in these industries. These sources are not easy to find, but they are often quoted in the more general books about social conditions in early Victorian times which are often available in public libraries. It may also be possible to find, especially in local libraries in the older industrial areas, studies by local historians which include material about industrial history. Where such material is available, it should prove possible to devise exercises like the ones suggested here – or more suitable ones.

THE IRISH POTATO FAMINE

Sources 24 and 25 are about the Irish potato famine and its sequel, which happened just after the writing of the portraits of industrial conditions in England which we have been considering. They will oblige us, as they obliged people in England at that time, to remember among their other preoccupations that Ireland too was part of Queen Victoria's realms.

Since 1801 Ireland had been a full part of the United Kingdom, but a very different part. Most of Ireland depended on the land, not on the new industries. Most of the people of Ireland were even poorer than the factory workers and farm labourers in England. Much of the country, especially the wet but beautiful mountainous west, was difficult to farm. There was also a big divide between three classes of people: the landlords (mainly English Protestants, some of whom did not even live in Ireland but had agents to run their estates); the tenant farmers (some Catholic and some Protestant, who did live there); and the peasants (nearly all Catholic, who worked for the farmers and in return held small patches of land on which to build a hut and grow their own crops and perhaps to keep a pig or two). Some of these peasants also made a little money by going each year to England and working there on farms, or as 'navvies' building canals and then railways.

Because farming of grain crops was so difficult they all benefited, especially those living in the west, from one crop which did grow well – the potato – which had been brought from the Americas in Tudor times. The success of potato growing enabled Ireland to be one of the most densely populated countries in Europe.

Then, beginning in 1845, came the disaster. Just as potatoes had crossed the Atlantic, so did a new and terrible blight, which turned a field of healthy potatoes into a stinking mass almost overnight. The blight appeared first in the eastern USA but then in Belgium and all across Europe. Ireland was one of the last countries to be affected. Source 24 tells what one of the landlords' agents felt like when the blight came to his land.

On August 6, 1846 – I shall not readily forget the day – I rode up as usual to my mountain property, and my feelings may be imagined when before I saw the crop, I smelt the fearful stench, now so well known and recognized as the death-sign of each field of potatoes . . . the luxuriant stalks soon withered, the leaves decayed, the disease extended to the tubers [parts of the potato plant which are eaten], and the stench from the rotting of such an immense amount of rich vegetable matter became almost intolerable . . .

But my own losses and disappointments, deeply as I felt them, were soon merged in the general desolation, misery, and starvation which now rapidly affected the poorer classes around me and throughout Ireland . . . The crop of all crops, on which they depended for food, had suddenly melted away, and no adequate arrangements had been made to meet this calamity – the extent of which was so sudden and so terrible that no one had appreciated it in time – and thus thousands perished almost without an effort to save themselves.

Source 24   Extract from W. Steuart Trench, *Realities of Irish Life*, 1868, describing his experiences of the potato famine (reproduced in Peter Gray, *The Irish Famine*, New Horizons series. London: Thames and Hudson, 1995, p. 139)

People who could grow other crops instead of potatoes began to do that. But in much of Ireland, and in the Highlands of Scotland too, there were no other crops. This was bad enough for landlords and their agents, but it was worse for the tenant farmers who had nothing to sell. It was still worse for the peasants, who had no food on their patches and no way of earning enough to buy food, because the farmers could not give them work and had no money to pay them.

There was a real danger that some people would starve. So some well-meaning philanthropists, especially Quakers, did what they could to help. The English Government of the day were slow to bother about Ireland, but they did pay out some money when pressure was put on them. But the blight happened more than once. The peasants became weak because of lack of food, and then ill with diseases. This made it more difficult for them to find the money for their rent.

Unfortunately, this happened at a time when the landlords wanted to get the peasants, and even the tenant farmers, off their land. If their estates were to pay, they had to farm them without bothering about small farms and smaller patches. So some of them took advantage of the debts, which the poorest people ran up, to 'evict'

them – turn them out of their homes – and sometimes to burn their huts down. Source 25 tells what one Quaker from York found during his travels in the far west, in County Mayo, during a visit in 1847.

Whilst upon the island of Achill [off the coast of County Mayo], I saw a memorable instance of this mode of proceeding [i.e. eviction of tenants and destruction of their cabins after the famine made it impossible for them to pay rent] . . . One old grey-haired man came tottering up to us, bearing in his arms his bed-ridden wife, and putting her down at our feet, pointed, in silent agony to her, and then to his roofless dwelling, the charred timbers of which were scattered in all directions around. This man said he owed little more than one year's rent, and had lived in the village, which had been the home of his forefathers, all his life. Another man, with five motherless children, had been expelled, and their 'boiling-pot' sold for 3s 6d. . . . From this village alone, at least one hundred and fifty persons had been evicted, owing from half a year's to a year and a half's rent. The whole of their effects, even the miserable furniture of these wretched cabins seized and sold to satisfy the claims of the nominal owner of Achill.

Source 25   Extract from James Hack Tate, *A visit to Connaught in the Autumn of 1847*, published in 1847 (reproduced in Peter Gray, *The Irish Famine*, New Horizons series. London: Thames and Hudson, 1995, pp. 141–2)

So what could the people do when they had been 'evicted'? Many died. Some rioted and burned down the farmers' houses. Some walked across Ireland to Dublin and, from the few shillings they had saved, bought a ticket to Liverpool and, having found work, settled there or in another of the big English cities. Some saved up until they could afford to emigrate by travelling 'steerage' (the cheapest class) to the USA or to Australia to seek a new life. Charities helped some of them in this emigration.

Ireland thus suffered a triple tragedy: famine,

eviction and emigration. Her population was reduced from about 8 million to about 5 million. To the English, Ireland's problems were a tiresome addition to the long list of her own troubles; something to be dealt with by a little charity, a little attention (Queen Victoria herself visited Dublin in 1849) and a little policing when there were riots. In fact it was a much more complicated story than has been indicated here, but this will give some idea of how important it was.

We can now see that what happened in the

1840s led to parts of some English and Scottish cities, and American and Australian cities, being mainly inhabited by Irish people, many of them Roman Catholics. It also made the misunderstandings between England and Ireland, and between the Catholics and Protestants in Ireland, worse. Since then, one way or another, politicians have never been able to forget about Ireland. If we are thinking about big social and political changes, the Irish Potato Famine was one of the most important events in Victoria's long reign.

SUGGESTED ACTIVITIES

With any class of children learning about the famine, it is necessary to decide how much background to include. The documents themselves will give a vivid instant impression. This could be supplemented by other material from the book from which these are taken – Peter Grey's *The Irish Famine.*

Possible activities might be:

- make up a play about how a peasant family heard about the blight from their neighbours and then one day found that it had destroyed

the crop on their own patch: describe that day
- compose a mural of peasants in front of their burned-down hut, ready to set out for Dublin: groups could each make a part of the mural
- make up a letter home, or a song, about their travels to Dublin and Liverpool and on to the New World
- can the children find out the names of famous American statesmen who can trace their ancestry back to Ireland?

QUEEN VICTORIA AND THE GREAT EXHIBITION, 1851

Queen Victoria herself has not figured widely in publications to help in the preparation of work on Victorian Britain (see Chapter 3, p. 25). Her journals or diaries are a minefield of personal information of interest to primary-age children. In Source 26 the long extract on the opening of the Great Exhibition in 1851 illustrates the Queen's interest in the economic development of Britain and the Empire. This shows her enthusiasm as a young woman of 32 and her praise for Prince Albert, who had been responsible for the Exhibition itself. The national

confidence in mid-century in the superiority of British exhibits is also clear from this source. The Crystal Palace, in which the Exhibition was housed, was a huge domed iron and glass building specially designed for the purpose by Joseph Paxton, and many countries were invited to exhibit their achievements. It was erected in Hyde Park, but later moved to south London where it remained for another century, finally being overcome by fire. The name 'Crystal Palace' lives on in the football team.

The confidence and enthusiasm of this

mid-Victorian period is shown by a speech given by Prince Albert in 1849 – the year of Queen Victoria's short visit to Ireland: 'The Exhibition of 1851 is to give us a true test and a living picture of the point of development at which the whole of mankind has arrived . . . and a new starting point from which all nations will be able to direct their further exertions'.

April 29, 1851 . . . *We drove to the Exhibition with only the 2 Maids of Honour and 2 Equerries and remained about 2 hours and ½. I came back quite dead beat and my head really bewildered by the myriads of beautiful and wonderful things, which now quite dazzle one's eyes. Such efforts have been made and our people have shown such taste in their manufactures, all owing to the impetus given by the Exhibition and by my beloved one's guidance. We went up into the Gallery, and the sight of it from there into all the Courts, full of all sorts of objects of art, manufacture etc. had quite the effect of fairyland . . .*

May 1 . . . *The Park presented a wonderful spectacle, crowds streaming through it – carriages and troops passing, quite like the Coronation, and for me, the same anxiety. The day was bright and all bustle and excitement. At ½ p. 11 the whole processing in 9 State carriages was set in motion . . . The Green Park and Hyde Park were one mass of densely crowded human beings, in the highest good humour and most enthusiastic . . . We drove up Rotten Row and got out of our carriages at the entrance on that side. The glimpse, through the iron gates of the Transept*, the waving palms and flowers, the myriads of people filling the galleries and seats around, together with the flourish of trumpets as we entered the building, gave a sensation I shall never forget and I felt much moved . . . In a few seconds we proceeded, Albert*

leading me, having Vicky at his hand and Bertie holding mine. The sight as we came to the centre where the steps and chair (on which I did not sit) was placed, facing the beautiful crystal fountain was magic and impressive. The tremendous cheering, the joy expressed in every face, the vastness of the building, with all its decorations and exhibits, the sound of the organ (with 200 instruments and 600 voices, which seemed nothing) and my beloved husband, the creator of this peace festival 'uniting the industry and art of all nations of the earth', all this was indeed moving, and a day to live for ever. God bless my dearest Albert, and my dear Country, which has shown itself so great today.

Source 26 Extracts from Queen's Victoria's journals (reproduced in D. Duff, *Victoria Travels*, Frederick Muller, 1970, p. 137)
*Since the Crystal Palace was built in the shape of a cross, like a cathedral, the 'entrance on (that) side' would open into a short lobby leading to the centre of the Exhibition and it was this lobby which Victoria, as Head of the Church of England, called a 'Transept', the term which would be used for a lobby like that in a cathedral.

Victoria's enthusiasm for and appreciation of the Great Exhibition of 1851 could be reflected in a piece of a similar nature by the children, describing their own experience of a visit to a place or an event which excited them. This should be closely related to their language work. For further information about the Great Exhibition one of the best resources, together with suggestions for activities about the Exhibition, is to be found in *Victorian Times*, by Jo Lawrie and Paul Noble (on pages 83–7). There, excellent advice is given for practical activities – for example, how to make a jigsaw puzzle of a picture of the Crystal Palace.

VICTORIAN SCHOOLS

Victorian schools is perhaps the most popular theme for primary schools, and much constructive help has come from publishers and museums. The topic provides immediacy when an old school celebrates its own centenary. Many whole-school exhibitions have been set up on these memorable occasions, especially during the 1980s, and often something of the resource material remains available.

Jo Lawrie, whose name has just been mentioned, is curator of Sevington School Museum, in a former village school in Wiltshire. She holds regular role-playing experiences at

VICTORIA.

Born May 24, 1819 ; began to reign June 20, 1837 ; married to her cousin, Prince Albert of Saxe-Coburg and Gotha, February 10, 1840. Princess Royal, born November 21, 1840. Prince of Wales, born November 9, 1841. Princess Alice, born April 25, 1843. Alfred Ernest Albert, born August 6, 1844. Princess Helena Augusta Victoria, born May 25, 1846. Louise Caroline Alberta, born March 18, 1848. Arthur Patrick Albert, born May 1, 1850. Leopold Duncan Albert, born April 7, 1853. Princess Beatrice Mary Victoria, born April 14, 1857.

This is the Sovereign fair and young,
Whose plaudits flow from every tongue.
Long may she reign, belov'd, in peace,
Each year her happiness increase.
Of all her ancient royal line,
May *hers* with noblest glories shine,
And bright in History's page be seen
VICTORIA'S name, our youthful Queen—

Source 27   Reference to Queen Victoria, from *Our Native England: or the Historical House that Jack Built, being the History of England Made Easy, in Familiar Verse, with 47 Woodcuts.* Price Sixpence. (London, Walter Smith, 1885. Re-issued by Sevington School, Sevington, near Chippenham, Wiltshire)

Sevington (see Joan Blyth, *History 5 to 11*). Her authentic resources at Sevington include a pocket-size book, small enough for little hands to hold, used to teach History to young children. It is entitled *Our Native England: History of England Made Easy*, and comprises sketches of all the Kings and Queens of England from the Saxon Egbert to Victoria's own time, with a poem under each. This was a kind of 'catechism' of English history, emphasising the importance of England, to be committed to memory. The teacher would then question the children on it, and they would have to give the 'right' answer. This little book was first published in 1838, one year after Victoria's accession, but was still in use in 1885! Source 27 is the page about Victoria herself, who was given more fulsome praise than any of her predecessors.

The information given in Source 27 is a good example of the love of facts without comment characteristic of many Victorian books. In this case it is a list of the nine royal children and their dates of birth (see Source 6, in Chapter 3). Rote-learning was needed if children were to memorise these facts with little understanding. Maybe this extract was also intended as an example to all women to have large families, at a time when many mothers and children died at childbirth or not long afterwards. Criticism of the Royal Family was allowed no place in children's education though it was not unknown among adults, notably when Victoria went into seclusion after Albert's death in 1861.

The second Sevington source for Victorian schooling is a list of rules for the school itself in Source 28, from *The Victorian Schoolday*, by W. Frankum and J. Lawrie.

The rules in Source 28 represent a stark comparison with schooling today. They assume that children will want to please their parents and teachers and that, when they do not, this will be a temporary lapse. The rules themselves are based on 'simple Bible teaching'. They would be

RULES FOR PUPILS.

I.
Prepare your lessons carefully.

II.
Come *regularly* and *punctually* to School.

III.
Be as *tidy* as possible in your dress.

IV.
If you do not understand what is taught, ask your Teacher to explain it.

V.
Be *respectful* and *attentive* to your Teachers, and remember how kind it is of them to take so much trouble with you.

VI.
Speak the *truth* at all costs.

VII.
Be respectful and obedient to your Parents, Guardians, Teachers, and all set over you.

VIII.
Study to be polite and courteous to all, avoiding coarseness and rudeness.

IX.
Fight against *selfishness*, *anger*, and *all* evil.

X.
Be kind and obliging to every one.

Source 28 Rules for pupils at Sevington School, Wiltshire (from Wynne Frankum and Jo Lawrie, *The Victorian Schoolday: a Teacher's Manual*, Wilts. County Council, 1992). See Bibliography.

displayed in every classroom, and they too would probably be learned by heart and tested by rote – another 'catechism'. It should be remembered that discipline was expected to be strict, and that all Head Teachers and many others habitually carried a cane and used it.

SUGGESTED ACTIVITIES

A pertinent activity would be to divide the class into three groups and to give each group a set length of time in which to learn

- the names of Queen Victoria's children, or
- the poem about the Queen, or
- the table of Rules for Pupils

A competition could be devised to see how many pupils in each group could write down from memory what they had learned. In the next session the three 'winners' could say their 'catechism' without notes. This would give the children the feel of being a Victorian child at school.

'Victorian schools' is a very suitable topic for study, on account of its easy comparison with children's everyday experience; because of the buildings and artefacts available in many schools; and above all because of museums such as Sevington School. *The Victorian Schoolday*, the book already mentioned, gives (on pages 71–2) a useful list of thirty-nine school museums, with addresses, from all over the country. One of the latest of these is the British School Museum at Hitchin, in a former establishment of the British and Foreign Schools Society, which exhibits the life-long collection by Jill Grey.

A rather different source for the study of late Victorian schools is an essay written by a thirteen-year-old girl in 1897, the year of the Queen's Diamond Jubilee. Source 29 shows her poor view of boys in general (but not of Willie Murphy).

I do not like boys. They are so rough and noisy. They think themselves much cleverer than girls but they are mistaken. Girls are much more useful to their mothers than boys. If you see a boy nursing a baby, he does it so clumsily you think all the time he is going to let it

drop. Boys make their sisters do all sorts of things, such as clean their boots, brush their clothes, put their playthings – bats, balls and marbles safely away. When a boy has tooth-ache he makes a deal more fuss about it than a girl would, and mother has to do a deal of things to make him quiet. Then boys are so fond of play that they cannot find time to come for their meals, and if they are not ready just when they want they make a row about it. The best thing to do then is to let them go without, and you may be sure that they will come to the bread and butter, before the bread and butter will go to them. It costs more to keep boys than girls, they wear out their boots so quickly and tear their clothes so dreadfully that the shoemaker and tailor are always calling at the house. Girls do not wear out half so many clothes. Folks say girls talk more than boys, but you should hear them at ball or marbles and then you would not think so. Well, I suppose there must be boys or we should have no one to build houses, plough the fields, look after gardens and shops. The nicest boy I know is Willie Murphy, he is a very nice fellow.

Source 29 From an essay by a girl aged 13, in 1897 (quoted in W. B. Stephens, *Teaching Local History*. Manchester: Manchester University Press, 1977, pp. 130–1)

Discussion of Source 29 could be started by the teacher reading the extract (watching carefully the class's reactions). The teacher could also challenge the class to write English as capably as this girl, little older than they are, managed a century ago. The next step could be to build up, on one part of the blackboard or its equivalent, a list of reasons for the girl's opinion of boys. Then a parallel list of defences that could have been made by the boys in 1897 could be placed alongside. From this, the whole question of bias in writing could be discussed, and deliberately biased as well as unbiased accounts could be written. There would probably be a clamour to compare this girl's account, and its rebuttal, with the situation today. Finally, it could be pointed out that there were, a century ago, children who did not conform to the frequently assumed gender stereotype of female acceptance of male superiority. (Perhaps this was a Suffragette in the making?)

VICTORIAN RAILWAYS

Many other topics could, of course, be broached in any encounter with this huge subject of Victorian Britain. For example, much could be made of the shipbuilding industry and merchant marine, on which so much of Britain's world trade depended in Victorian times. But no survey would be really complete without some reference to the profound influence of the new railways on social and economic life. The 'railway age' is conventionally dated from the Liverpool and Manchester Railway, opened in 1830, seven years before Victoria came to the throne. By 1837 the network had expanded considerably – in that year the London and Birmingham Railway was opened – and soon covered most of the country, becoming the normal way by which passengers and freight were carried.

These railways also reflected the divisions in society. At first, third-class passengers rode in open-air trucks, sitting on hard wooden seats, enduring the noise and dirt of the new steam locomotives while first-class travellers enjoyed larger seats, more space and luxurious upholstery in enclosed carriages. Second-class travel came between the other two. Later, all carriages were enclosed, but third-class passengers were not allowed on some of the best trains until the 1880s. By that time, rail travel was a normal experience for most people. Then, especially when most people's working ended at mid-day on Saturday, cheap excursions to the seaside were introduced.

As time passed, bigger and better-designed locomotives led to heavier and faster trains. Water-troughs were introduced to enable locomotives to pick up water without stopping. Rivalries between companies were sometimes intense, and so risks were taken, sometimes resulting in serious accidents.

One famous rivalry was on the London–Scotland railways. Well-to-do people from London, who could afford long rail journeys in comfort, travelled north to take part in the 'grouse shoot' after 12 August each year. In 1890 the (rail) Forth Bridge, west of Edinburgh, was finished, and this enabled the 'East Coast route' to Aberdeen to compete more effectively with the 'West Coast route'. The East Coast route was now shorter (523 miles, as against 540 for the West Coast) and flatter: the West Coast had to contend with the Shap and Beattock summits. But the West Coast people had the best locomotives, could pick up water from 'troughs', and had only one change-over point at Carlisle. Meanwhile the East Coast route involved three companies, needed changes at York and Edinburgh, had more sharp turns, in the part north of the Border, and was particularly slow between Arbroath and Montrose.

Map 1 shows the two routes and the companies who ran them. In August 1885 the rival companies, looking for publicity, ran a famous series of overnight Railway Races: the winner was the first past the signal box at Kinnaber Junction, some miles south of Aberdeen, where the two routes joined.

Sources 30 and 31 help to capture the atmosphere of those Railway Races, just over a century ago, and to show how important people thought the railways were. The first, Source 30, comes from a newspaper called *The Standard*. It describes the last race from London to Aberdeen contested by both competitors, and appears to be an unbiased account. (Of course the newspapers came out the day after the race: 22 August for the race overnight on 20–21 August, and so on.)

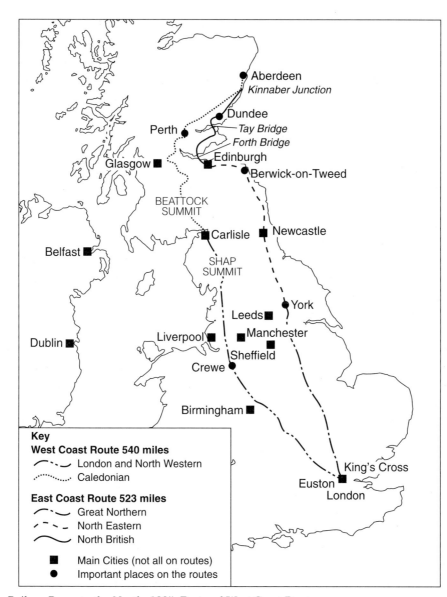

Map 1 The Railway Races to the North, 1895. East and West Coast Routes

There was again a fierce contest on the East and West Coast Routes yesterday morning in the great railway race to the North. Both trains started punctually at eight o'clock on Tuesday night from Euston and King's Cross, and some splendid running on both routes was accomplished. The West Coast train, however, gained the day, steaming into Aberdeen Station at 4.58 yesterday morning, the journey of 540 miles having been accomplished in 8 hours 58 minutes. Several spurts were run at 64 miles an hour. The East Coast train did not arrive until 5.11 which, however, beats all previous records on this route by 21 minutes. Both trains were well filled with passengers. It will be seen that the West Coast train covered the entire distance at the rate of 60 miles an hour with two minutes to spare.

Source 30 Extract from the *Standard*, 22 August 1895 (quoted in O. S. Nock, *The Railway Race to the North*, Ian Allan, 1959 (1976 edition), p. 112)

The second extract, Source 31, comes from another newspaper, *The Sketch*, and is about the last, record-breaking, run. It describes the prowess of Driver Soutar, of the Caledonian Railway – the 'Cally' – with its vivid blue locomotives, which operated the northern end of the West Coast Route. Soutar was greatly acclaimed by the waiting crowd at Aberdeen. The hard work of his 'stoker', feeding coal into the fire-box on the locomotive, helped Soutar to keep up an average speed of 66.8 miles per hour on the final lap from Perth to Aberdeen: 63.3 miles per hour on the whole Euston–Aberdeen run, then – and for long afterwards – the fastest in the world over such a distance. (Observers from the New York Central Railroad came specially to watch. Remember that until the following year, 1896, cars on British public roads could not exceed 4 mph and had to be preceded by a man with a red flag.)

Driver Soutar, who has all along been in charge of this engine, is the railway hero of the moment. Soutar, who is nearly sixty-one, joined the service as a fireman forty-four years ago. He has conveyed the Queen to the North on many occasions with this very engine. There was much excitement at Aberdeen on the great day, the train being waited for by a crowd of spectators. Soutar and his stoker were borne shoulder-high and presented with a couple of blue ribbons. A unique result of the race was that letters which left London by the eight o'clock evening train were sent out in Aberdeen by the first morning delivery.

Source 31   Extract from the *Sketch*, 23 August 1895 (quoted in O. S. Nock, *The Railway Race to the North*, Ian Allan, 1959 (1976 edition), p. 121). This was the final lap of the record run. Note the almost obligatory reference to the Queen, in the 58th year of her reign.

And who won the Races as a whole? Most, but not all, of those August races were won by the West Coast. So was that last actual race, on the night of 20–21 August but, as Source 30 points out, the East Coast crew also achieved their fastest average time so far on that night: it was 56.7 miles per hour instead of 54.8. All the same, the managements of the East Coast companies then decided that it was too expensive and perhaps dangerous to try to win again; so they did not run on the next night, 21–22 August. But the West Coast companies did, and that was when they set up their record, with Driver Soutar on the last lap. So we have to say that the West Coast won.

SUGGESTED ACTIVITIES

The two 'railway races' sources could be used in different ways according to the age of the class. In any case a teacher would first give a quick verbal sketch of how the railway system grew: there are many useful books about this, and some of them have maps, on some of which the two routes to the North may be found. One possibility for some classes would be to use outline maps of Great Britain, with the routes on our sketch-map and dots for the main places marked, and then to add the names of the places from an atlas. If necessary, a blackboard map could be used to help here. This could be related to the learning of the shape of the British Isles required in the Geography curriculum.

Children could write imaginative accounts from the point of view of:

- a passenger on one of the racing trains
- a spectator waiting at Aberdeen in the early morning of 22 August 1895, to see which train came in first
- Driver Soutar, about his run during the night of 21–22 August.

Another useful possibility, for children who have sufficient attainment in 'number', would be for them to work out, from the figures given in the text, the average speeds in miles per hour, including the record 63.3. Some children may be interested in technical details about gauges, locomotive wheel patterns, rolling stock, time-tables (the 'Bradshaws' were well established by the 1890s), or other technical details. They may also like to learn about the individual companies with their imposing and influential Chairmen and Chief Mechanical Engineers: many of those railways have their own histories available in public libraries. Some children of junior age are fascinated by records of one sort or another, and might like to compare that record of 63.3 mph with the performance over similar distances of modern trains in, for example, France or Japan, or with land-speed car records. If children have any of these interests, then they could undertake further work on some of these – provided that they also explain it to the rest of the class.

USING VICTORIAN SOURCES

Using Victorian sources presents fewer difficulties than in the case of earlier periods where documents are less accessible and harder to read. So older juniors, in particular, can work directly on these documents individually or in pairs. For all classes the teacher could use the whole of the documents, or parts of them, in preparing class teaching. It is advisable to encourage children to find books on the Victorians at the beginning of a study, to be used in written work at the end. Most of the established publishers such as Longman, Collins, Hodder and Stoughton, Oxford University Press and Ginn have produced pupils' books and teachers' resources for the National Curriculum, and there are many good information books published since 1992. More detailed books are needed for specific purposes such as the technology of the textile or other industry, for school life particularly in the public schools not discussed here, and for Queen Victoria's private life at Osborne House in the Isle of Wight (see Chapter 3).

As has already been shown, there is considerable scope for work in pairs and groups on sub-topics, leading to class discussions considering different points of view. Visits too should be made if the locality allows, to textile and other museums, to 'live' classrooms at Sevington and elsewhere such as Wigan Pier, and to transport museums including the National Railway Museum at York. The study can culminate in a class exhibition, a procedure which allows considerable variety according to the nature of the work. For younger juniors, especially, role-play can figure more prominently. In all this work, it is once again important to emphasise the big social changes which took place *during* Victoria's long reign, and also 'then-now' comparisons with life today.

VICTORIAN NOVELS

No chapter on Victorian written sources would be complete without some reference to Victorian novels, either to give contemporary atmosphere, as in those by Charles Dickens, or to delineate real or imagined characters in the past (or both). Chapter 10 concentrates on twentieth-century novelists writing for children, mostly since 1950, their books being published in paperback for children to buy. Before that date, there were only a few such books. Historical novels were mostly hardback and expensive.

Post-1950 books have usually been written by novelists keen to ensure the historical accuracy of their writing. Earlier novels were often exciting, but with less attention paid to veracity. Therefore teachers must be more cautious in their selection of earlier historical fiction. In any case, few of those historical novels or biographies were written for *primary* children.

In selecting pre-1950 books for their own or their pupils' reading, teachers should observe the advice of specialists. Helen Cam, in a seminal pamphlet on *Historical Novels*, stressed the importance of novels for students of History because of their characterisation of ordinary people – 'history is about human beings'. Sir John Marriott (*English History in English Fiction*) considered that novels are a starting-point for all historians – 'the novelist's business is not to satisfy but to stimulate historical curiosity'. Primary-school children can make this introduction, later to be 'satisfied', or at least nurtured, by more systematic study of history in the secondary school. These two well-known academic historians give sound advice on which novels constitute 'good' history.

Although historical novels are written by adults for adults, many are still read by children, often in abridged or cartoon form. Charles Dickens' *Oliver Twist* and *Nicholas Nickleby* depict the 'way of life' of street children and of those sent to brutal private boarding schools. They are illuminating about aspects of nineteenth-century life and were a form of 'whistle-blowing' much needed at that time. The same applied to Charles Kingsley's *Water Babies*, revealing the cruelty of life as a 'climbing boy' (chimney sweep). Kingsley also wrote a best-seller about Elizabethan seamen in *Westward Ho!* (1855). Thomas Hughes' *Tom Brown's Schooldays* reveals that those schooldays, like Nicholas Nickleby's, were hardly 'the happiest days' of life for either the rich or those of more limited means: the extracts about Sevington School in this chapter (Sources 27 and 28) show that the children of the rural labouring

poor also had a hard time of it.

Silas Hocking's *Her Benny* (1879), a sentimental story of two Liverpool waifs, shows that life begging in the streets was even worse than life in school. The sources on factories and mines (Sources 22 and 23) can be supplemented by reading from two novels written from an adult point of view: Benjamin Disraeli's *Sybil, or the Two Nations* (1845), in which Sybil, a factory girl, and a wealthy young man fall in love with each other, and Elizabeth Gaskell's *Mary Barton* (1848), which also depicts the hardships of industrial life in the mid-century. For late Victorian times, a general impression of urban life in the Midlands and North of England is conveyed with particular vividness in Arnold Bennett's novels about the Potteries published just after the Victorian age, notably *Anna of the Five Towns* (1902), *The Old Wives' Tale* (1908) and *Clayhanger* (1910).

These novels are not recommended reading for the majority of primary *pupils*, but there are ways in which teachers can usefully use them. For one thing, they can read them for their own interest and to absorb 'background' for their teaching. They can also encourage good readers in Year 6 (and in middle schools, Years 7 and 8) to read such novels. For this purpose it is necessary to press for the inclusion of copies in the school library, and also to encourage the development of the habit of using public libraries, so that, in an age so easily dependent on television, the use of written sources of this kind can become a lifelong habit.

SEVEN

Britain Since 1930

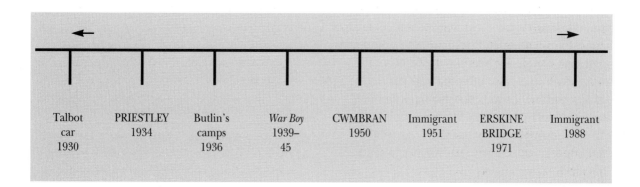

| Talbot car 1930 | PRIESTLEY 1934 | Butlin's camps 1936 | *War Boy* 1939–45 | CWMBRAN 1950 | Immigrant 1951 | ERSKINE BRIDGE 1971 | Immigrant 1988 |

This topic, covering the twentieth century and soon to overlap into the twenty-first, presents more difficulties in selection of original sources than does Victorian Britain. This may be because it is too near us to be seen in perspective. Any list of sources may be too vague or too specific for juniors to understand. In this period of visual and oral appeal it is surprisingly difficult to find short, vivid sources appealing to primary-age children. Since the introduction of the National Curriculum in 1991, teachers in England, supported by publishers, have apparently considered it safer to concentrate on a few topics including World War Two, especially on 'evacuation' in 1939–40, on the blitz on cities in 1940–41 and on flying bombs in the South of England in 1944–45. In actual fact, more lasting changes than these have taken place in society since 1945 which affect more children of today for a longer time.

We have therefore selected ten less well-known or less accessible sources. These are: the motor car; the 1939–45 war on the coast; immigration; holidays; New Towns; and new links in the road system. As a reminder that this topic is 'Britain Since 1930', we have chosen a New Town in Wales and a new road bridge in Scotland. The time line *Victoria to the Present Day* and the twentieth-century *Family Pack*, published by Pictorial Charts Educational Trust are helpful for children to view the period 1930 to 1990 as whole, in a slightly longer time-context.

J. B. PRIESTLEY

We start with two sources from a survey of much of England made in 1934: J. B. Priestley's *English* *Journey*. This was one of a long line of descriptions of travels through England. There were examples in Tudor times (John Leland, William Camden and William Harrison – see Source 19) but most of them were written in years not included in the National Curriculum for Key Stage 2. So Priestley followed a distinguished tradition. He was of course a well-known author and playwright and a distinctive socialist thinker, but *English Journey* is a unique portrait of the 1930s, coloured by his general views. It is worthwhile for teachers in any school to look up what Priestley has to say about their own region, for he went almost everywhere except the south-east and south-west. Source 32 is chosen because it shows how Blackpool in 1934 had changed from the days before World War One and expressed what was then regarded as new, modern, and slightly too Americanised for Priestley's liking.

They [the people of Blackpool] would turn it into a pleasure resort for the crowd, and especially the Lancashire crowd from the cotton mills. Blackpool should give them what they wanted . . . Blackpool did. Compared with this huge mad place, with its miles and miles of promenades, its three piers, its gigantic dance-halls, its variety shows, its switch-backs and helter-skelters, its array of wine bars and oyster saloons and cheap restaurants and tea houses and shops piled high and glittering with trash; its army of pierrots, bandsmen, clowns, fortune-tellers, auctioneers, dancing partners, animal trainers, itinerant singers, hawkers; its seventy special trains a day, its hundreds and hundreds of thousands of trippers; places like Brighton and Margate and Yarmouth are merely playing at being popular resorts. Blackpool has them all licked. It has recently built a bathing pool that does not hold mere hundreds of people but thousands, the population of a small town. It has decided that it ought to extend its season into October, while the beds are still aired and the frying-pans hot, and so now every autumn it has the whole front, miles of it, illuminated with coloured lights, not a few thousand coloured lights but hundreds of thousands of them. That is Blackpool.

[But] Its amusements are becoming too mechanised and Americanised. Talkies have replaced the old roaring variety turns. Gangs of carefully drilled young men and women (with nasal accents), employed by the music publishers to 'plug' their 'Hot Broadway Hits', have largely replaced the pierrots and . . . . . . minstrels. The entertainers are more calculating, their shows more standardised, and the audiences more passive. It has developed a pitiful sophistication – machine-made and not really English – that is much worse than the old hearty vulgarity.

Source 32 Extracts from J. B. Priestley, *English Journey* (originally published by Heinemann, 1934, reprinted by Mandarin Paperbacks, 1994, pp. 265–6 and 267)

It is useful to compare this snapshot of the holiday Mecca of much of northern England and southern Scotland with Source 35 which is about Billy Butlin and his holiday camps, begun about the same time.

Towards the end of the book, Priestley reflected more generally on what he had seen and felt during his journey about the England of that time. He traced the survival of an older, upper-class world and a traditional working-class culture, but saw both being overtaken by a new post-war way of life. This is expressed in Source 33. It is included in order to convey a sense of perspective. To us, the 1930s is 'pre-war'. To him, it was 'post-war', though he could see the clouds gathering again. It is useful to remember this when looking at change in Britain since 1930.

[This] was the new post-war England, belonging far more to the age itself than to this particular island. America, I supposed, was its real birth-place. This is the England of arterial and by-pass roads, of filling stations and factories that look like exhibition buildings, of giant cinemas and dance-halls and cafés, bungalows with tiny garages, cocktail bars, Woolworths, motor-coaches, wireless, hiking, factory girls looking like actresses, greyhound racing and dirt

tracks, swimming pools, and everything given away for cigarette coupons . . . You need money in this England, but you do not need much money. It is a large-scale, mass-production job, with cut prices. You could almost accept Woolworths as its symbol . . . In this England, for the first time in history, Jack and Jill are nearly as good as their master and mistress; they may have always been as good in their own way, but now they are nearly as good in the same way. Jack, like his master, is rapidly transported to some place of rather mechanical amusement. Jill beautifies herself exactly as her mistress does. It is an England, at last, without privilege. Years and years ago the democratic and enterprising Blackpool, by declaring that you were all as good as one another so long as you have the necessary sixpence, began all this. Modern England is rapidly Blackpooling itself . . . The very modern things, like the films and wireless and sixpenny stores . . . are absolutely democratic . . . you get neither more nor less than what everybody else gets.

Source 33 Extract from J. B. Priestley, *English Journey* (originally published by Heinemann, 1934, and re-issued by Mandarin Paperbacks, 1994, pp. 401–2)

It is valuable to reflect on how much of that 'new' Britain still looks new, and how much now seems archaic. Work with children on both documents could concentrate on what changes have taken place since Priestley wrote: a chart with 'Then' and 'Now' headings could be made by individuals, or by the class. For children who go, or have been, to Blackpool, there is particular scope. Others could compare Blackpool with other British resorts, or with what counts as attraction on the Costa Brava or Disneyland or elsewhere, and could write a description of this, to be read by young children doing history in 2050 or thereabouts. If it proves possible to locate a copy of *English Journey*, there could be added interest through the judicious use of extracts about the schools' own region.

THE MOTOR CAR

The next example concentrates on the motor car, which came to be an essential means of transport for most people, overtaking the train as it became cheaper and handier. For this topic the written and visual source provided is an advertisement for the Talbot 'Foursome' coupé shown in *The Motor* for 21 October 1930, and reproduced as Source 34.

The picture gives clues for the costumes and interests of the upper middle class in the early 1930s, when for most people the Great Depression, whose social effects Priestley deplored, was still very much in evidence. So we see the trilby hat and stick for the gentleman, the fur collar and fur coat-bottom for the lady, and the popularity of the wire-haired terrier. Even the snappy brand name 'Foursome' indicates that this dashing coupé was intended for young people who went about in pairs or couples and were used

to, and could afford, golf and bridge. The female driver too was a recent and rather daring development. The written part of the document outlines the luxury of the coupé car, with its fold-back hood, affording room for five people and their luggage, adjustable front seats and arm-rests (but of course no seat-belts). The advertised price was in the luxury range: the popular Ford and Morris models sold for between £100 and £200.

This document about the motor car can figure in part of a topic on twentieth-century transport. Materials can be obtained from transport museums and from the one specially devoted to cars: Beaulieu Motor Museum in Hampshire. Other helpful sources are the transport sections in public libraries, and historical articles in magazines such as *The Motor*, including descriptions of past annual Motor Shows in London. These sources could lead to individual

And now the TALBOT "Foursome" Coupé

SO absolutely *right* was the "Foursome" Collapsible Coupe (as designed by Pass and Joyce over three years ago) that its popularity has increased beyond measure. The new designs with their unique grace and powerful sweeping lines are exclusive.

On the new Talbot chassis the "Foursome" is a perfect example of elegance and efficiency. The head is raised or lowered with the greatest ease, there is room for four or five to be comfortably seated, and a roomy luggage boot is included. Write for further particulars of this fascinating Coupe.

The "Foursome" Coupe :

Full Drop-head
Weymann or Coachbuilt
construction
Exterior and interior
finish to choice
Pneumatic upholstery
Adjustable front seats
Folding armrests to
rear seat
Winding windows
Roomy luggage boot
Perfect driving visibility
First-class workmanship

Talbot Collapsible
"Foursome" Coupe

from **£695**

SEE PASS AND JOYCE AT OLYMPIA
STAND 33

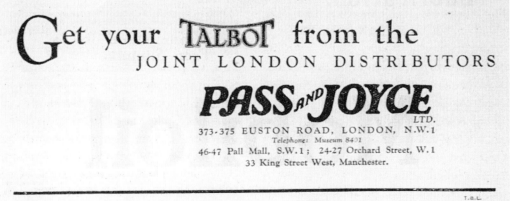

Get your TALBOT from the
JOINT LONDON DISTRIBUTORS

PASS AND JOYCE LTD.

373-375 EUSTON ROAD, LONDON, N.W.1
Telephone: Museum 8401
46-47 Pall Mall, S.W.1; 24-27 Orchard Street, W.1
33 King Street West, Manchester.

KINDLY MENTION "THE MOTOR" WHEN CORRESPONDING WITH ADVERTISERS.

T.&L.
F39

Source 34 Advertisement for Talbot 'Foursome' Coupé, 1930, from *The Motor*, 21 October 1930. Reproduced by kind permission of Peugeot Motor Company PLC; Photograph courtesy of National Motor Museum written work based on discussion of what the advertisement reveals about social life in England in the period. Incidentally, any work of this kind will help children's current vocabulary: *pneumatic; visibility*. It might be useful to lead children to make their own, modern, posters, based on what they see on hoardings and on TV, and then to talk about then/now differences both in advertising and marketing, and in the cars themselves, of which most will have had family experience, whereas most juniors in the 1930s did not. Modern advertising aims at a wider social market, but the firms making cars today are almost all foreign-owned. This can in turn lead to discussion of environmental issues such as the extension of motorways and bridge links (see also Map 3 and Sources 40 and 41) and traffic congestion, and also, where appropriate, to the changing technology of the internal combustion engine and of car bodies and chassis.

LEISURE PURSUITS

The next topic is the growth of leisure pursuits: it is of course related to what Priestley had said about Blackpool. As people came to have more disposable income, and as cheap transport (first 'charabancs' and coaches as well as trains, and then private cars) became more available than even in Victorian times, the expansion of leisure opportunities became more marked. As outlined in the 1995 Order for English National Curriculum History, radio, cinema, sport, and then television are suggested as topics: each is obviously enormous in its scope.

Here, we have selected seaside holidays, and in particular the distinctive kind of holiday camp owned by Billy Butlin and his organisation. Soon after World War Two, these camps with their cheap but sound accommodation and ready-made amusements, became an annual experience for many families in different parts of the country. Butlin's camps, and later others such as Pontin's, were erected mainly near seaside locations such as Skegness, Minehead, Ayr in Scotland and Pwllheli in North Wales. Families who had never had a holiday away from home during the Depression years of the 1930s or during the War, tried this new experience. At first, newcomers to a camp did not mix well, for they were unused to talking to 'strange people' from other parts of the country. But soon they became used to their annual Butlin's visit, and to re-uniting with old friends.

What we needed was some way of getting the campers to mix. On the third day of that first week I said to Norman Bradford, 'How about livening them up a bit?' So after dinner that night he went on stage in his usual jovial manner, joked with the campers and told them about the various facilities and activities. Then he said 'Now I want everyone to turn to the person on your right, introduce yourself and shake hands.' There was a bit of embarrassment at first, but people did so, laughing and smiling shyly. 'Now', continued Norman, 'turn to the person on your left and do the same.' This time people did it with more gusto and friendliness. The ice had been broken. Throughout the dining-room people began talking to each other. This made a great difference in the atmosphere of the place.

'This is what we've been missing,' I said to myself. 'A few more friendly people around, like Norman, would work wonders.' . . . 'Go and buy yourself a blazer,' I told Norman. He returned with one in blue, primrose yellow and white – the camp's colour scheme. But somehow it did not seem quite right. I did not want an outfit that looked like a uniform, for that would have given the wrong impression. What I was searching for was something bright, cheerful and holiday-looking. This line of thought led me to choose a red blazer and white flannels. We had them made by a local tailor and before the first week was over Norman bounced on to the stage at breakfast wearing the outfit. 'Good morning, campers,' he shouted.

'Good morning,' everyone shouted back. As I heard this reaction I felt a flutter of excitement . . .

Source 35   Extract from B. Butlin and P. Dacre, *A Showman to the End* (London: Robson Books, 1982, p. 195, reprinted in *Butlin's Student Guide*, revised edition, Butlin's Holidays, 1995). The extract refers to the first 'Butlin's Luxury Holiday Camp' at Skegness, Easter 1936. Norman Bradford was the camp's Master of Ceremonies

The extract in Source 35 comes from an autobiography of Billy Butlin himself, written with P. Dacre: *A Showman to the End*. It describes how Norman Bradford, Master of Ceremonies at Skegness, got the 'campers' to be sociable on Easter Saturday 1936. This style of a friendly, noisy community, as well as good food provided for tired housewives and on-the-spot entertainment for all the family, became the hallmark of Butlin's camps and of their rivals. These camps are still running, but since the 1970s cheap package holidays abroad have made the camps relatively less popular. But recollections by family, friends or neighbours of the great days of the camps, or even a visit to a nearby camp if there is one, might still be possible for juniors. In any case teacher-led discussions, using maps and books, could arouse enough interest for children to seek out more details of songs, games, celebrations, food and bungalows at the camps, and in the process to see how recent history can be brought to life.

WAR ON THE COAST

Source 36, illustrating war on the coast, is taken from the artist Michael Foreman's exquisite autobiography *War Boy*. The scene was a Suffolk coastal village, too near a naval target at Lowestoft to avoid being bombed by German planes. Michael's mother kept a shop and served the many British, Commonwealth and (later) American troops stationed in the vicinity. Into this personal story the paraphernalia of the home front – gas masks, Anderson shelters, ration books and the rest – come naturally, and the artist's own illustrations give clear and often amusing colour to the narrative. The extract chosen is about an air raid.

I woke up when the bomb came through the roof. It came through at an angle, overflew my bed by inches, bounced up over my mother's bed, hit the mirror, dropped into the grate and exploded up the chimney. It was an incendiary. A fire-bomb. My brother Ivan appeared in pyjamas and his Home Guard tin hat. Being in the Home Guard, he had ensured that all the rooms in our house were stuffed with sandbags. Ivan threw sand over the bomb but the dry sand kept sliding off. He threw the hearthrug over the bomb and jumped up and down on it, until brother Pud arrived with a bucket of wet sand from the yard. This did the trick.
Mother grabbed me from the bed. The night sky was filled with lights. Searchlights, anti-aircraft fire, stars and a bombers' moon. The sky bounced as my mother ran. Just as we reached our dug-out across the street, the sky flared red as the church exploded . . . It was Monday, April 21, 1941, just before 10 p.m. . . . We were safe . . .

In the morning we returned home. Mum went to the loo, which was outside in the yard, and found a hole in the roof and a bomb, unexploded, in the floor. Pud pulled it out and carried it to 'Pal', the policeman in the police box on the corner.

Source 36   Extracts from Michael Foreman, *War Boy* (London: Pavilion Books Ltd, 1989, pp. 7, 8, 11, 12 and 14) describing a raid on a village near Lowestoft, 'Britain's nearest town to Germany'

War Boy offers a vivid story to be read to younger juniors, and by older juniors. This in turn can give rise to imaginative writing of the 'I was there' kind. But it is important to avoid allowing imagination to run riot without insisting on historical accuracy, which in turn involves looking up relevant background in the many lively information books about World War Two. Incidentally, *War Boy* shows how cigarette cards from 1939–45 can be used as a source – for example, Churchman's cards carried a sequence illustrating how to use a stirrup pump. In addition, some schools might compare this wartime 'country childhood' with different scenes in 1939–45: the almost untouched countryside farther away from the East Coast, but also the far greater intensity of aerial bombardment in most of the great cities.

A good basis for role-playing would be Mrs Foreman's General Store, with soldiers from many countries talking about the war with Michael and his two brothers, careful to obey orders that 'careless talk costs lives': what sort of thing would they be able to say without giving anything away to Hitler's war machine? The Imperial War Museum and many well-known publishers provide books, pictures, tapes and packs in which some material suitable for children at Key Stage 2 can be found. There is important scope too for then/now comparisons of life in different parts of the country including Scotland and Wales and Northern Ireland,

bringing out the traumatic upheavals brought about by World War Two and the immense changes during the children's own grandparents' and parents' lives. In such ways the impact of World War Two can be more fully conveyed than through evacuation and the blitz.

Part of the re-planning of British life after World War Two included the establishment of New Towns. Slums had been a marked feature of life in cities and towns before 1939, and social reformers had begun to tear them down and re-house the people in estates nearer the countryside. Many children now live in these inter-war estates. During World War Two, many of the slum areas had been badly damaged by German bombs, because they were near the centres of the cities and towns. After the war, too, families grew in size and needed still more houses. So once again people were often moved out to the edge of the cities and towns. But now there was also a movement to establish entirely New Towns, well designed, with an identity of their own. This idea was not new: towns such as Letchworth, Welwyn Garden City and Port Sunlight had already been established. But after the Town Planning Act of 1946, many more New Towns were planned, not only for 'slum clearance' but as part of a new Britain.

CWMBRAN NEW TOWN

The example we have chosen is Cwmbran New Town, (in Welsh, strictly, Cwmbrân: pronounced *Coom-brahn*: means 'Valley of the Crow) in south-east Wales, which dates from 1950–51. Map 2 shows its location.

Like all the other New Towns, Cwmbran had its own Development Corporation which drew up a Development Plan, technical in nature and unappealing to the lay reader (let alone primary-age children). But Cwmbran's Corporation also produced a readable booklet from which Source 37 is taken.

In the Eastern Valley of Monmouthshire are sited some of the most important industries in the county. There is practically no unemployment in this area . . . From other parts of the county people travel as far as 18 miles every day to work in these industries. It is largely . . . to house the people near the industries in which they work . . . that a new town is to be built at Cwmbran, roughly midway between Newport and Pontypool.

The present population of the area is about 13,000. Road and rail communications are good, which fact,

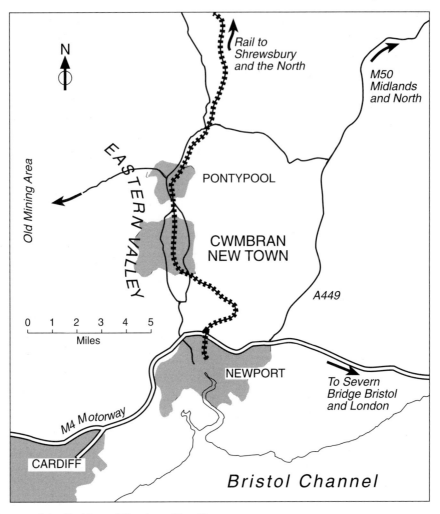

Map 2   Sketch map of the Position of Cwmbran New Town

taken in conjunction with the availability of suitable sites, has resulted in many factories being built within the area . . . There are large tracts of derelict land, sites of abandoned clay pits for the brick works, and old colliery workings. The remainder of the area is chiefly farm land of medium quality – and small scattered woodlands.

Out of this hotch-potch of houses, industries, waste land and farm land the Cwmbran Development Corporation has been given the task of creating an integrated township with a population of 35,000; a self-contained community with its own industries, commercial premises and shops, its own schools,

cultural and religious centres, and facilities for amusement and recreation.

Source 37   Extracts from *Cwmbran New Town: Abridged Report on Master Plan* (Cwmbran Development Corporation, c.1951, pp. 5–6)

The first part of the extract in Source 37 states what sort of New Town was planned for Cwmbran, and what features of the district the planners thought important to take into account. That district was just east of the South Wales coalfield, in what is known as the Eastern Valley. As the source shows, there were already existing industries and the New Town was to be a dormitory for their workers. The second part shows what sort of place they expected Cwmbran to become. At that time, many people considered that they could predict fairly accurately the 'brave new world' that was to be built after the war.

Now almost half a century has passed since Cwmbran New Town was established and there have in fact been many changes since then.

- Plans for the different neighbourhoods were not all implemented at once: much depended on ease of building.
- One tower block of flats was built near the centre, to act as a landmark and focus for the town.
- A steelworks was built nearby, in 1958, needing many more workers and houses.
- An industrial park was established, housing factories for car brakes, valves, nylon spinning, biscuit-making, and some other kinds of engineering.
- After about 1970, the older heavy industries, including the steelworks, became less prosperous.
- Then the new road network (M4 across the Severn Bridge and M50–A40 and A449 nearby) made for better access. Also the Newport–Shrewsbury railway through Cwmbran survived as a main route.
- New high-technology industries replaced the older ones and needed highly-skilled workers.
- The figure for expected population was then raised from 35,000 to 50,000, so that workers for the new industries could live near their work. (In fact, many chose to drive to work from farther away.)
- The shopping patterns originally intended – neighbourhood shops, town-centre shops and mobile shops to go round the neighbourhoods – were substantially modified by popular supermarkets with accessible free parking, which attracted people from Newport and Pontypool.
- There was a need for more leisure activities, especially for young people. But one of the first

ideas, for a 'river park' along the Afon Lwyd, has survived. Changes like these have happened in many places including other New Towns.

Much of this information was helpfully provided by the Torfaen (pronounced Tor-vine) County Borough Council which now manages Cwmbran's affairs. They have produced a *Factpack* for local schools which can be more widely used, especially in English schools in the Bristol–Gloucester area. There is also a book about the history of Cwmbran New Town, published by the Development Corporation: *Rebuilding a Valley*, by Philip Riden.

Suitable activities could be arranged by teachers for work in pairs. Older children could help to plan their own work. Cwmbran can give rise to useful links with geography (*settlement* as a theme, and a possible *contrasting locality*) and can afford examples of *economic and industrial understanding* and *environmental education*.

Questions to be considered include:

- Why was Cwmbran New Town established, and how was it expected to develop?
- How has Cwmbran changed since 1950?
- Think of a New Town near where you live. Is it like Cwmbran? Are there any differences?
- If possible, arrange to interview older residents in your New Town who have moved there since it was established. Ask what they expected when they moved, and whether that has happened.
- Think of your own town/suburb/estate/village. Find out, from people who live there, what changes have taken place since 1950. Are these changes like the ones in Cwmbran.
- Observe, in your own place, buildings erected at different times, and make a chart with photos or drawings to show what they looked like. (Styles of building change rapidly, even in New Towns.)
- What changes would you like to see in your area before 2020? This should give rise to teacher-led discussion.

IMMIGRATION

The next two of our post-war sources are concerned with the immigration of non-white peoples into Britain. Men and women from the countries of the British Commonwealth came initially to fight in World War Two. Then, in the immediate post-war years, immigrants were welcomed to undertake low-paid work, particularly in the building industry, as part of post-war reconstruction. Transport in the big cities, and the textile industries which then maintained an export trade, then later nursing continued to absorb immigrant labour until the 1950s. But no special provision was made to house these newcomers, who competed with white people in the general shortage of accommodation, and were therefore resented. The first source, Source 38, illustrates this competition for somewhere to live and is taken from *Race and Borough Politics* by Frank Reeves. A Jamaican immigrant interviewed long afterwards, in 1981, spoke of the discrimination he encountered when looking for accommodation in 1951.

When I first came here the most difficult part was to find a place to live. At that time the white people weren't quick to have you in their homes. I went to several places looking for a room, but I couldn't get one. One day I walked all day. I got a job first before I got a place. I was taken to the Labour Exchange and they gave me a card and sent me to [a prominent local employer] – they gave me a job right away. It said where did I live. I couldn't put an address on it so I just put my friend's address where I was stopping for that time until the following day when I walked round again.

Source 38   Extract from an oral record by a Jamaican looking back from the 1980s to his arrival in England in the 1950s (quoted in F. Reeves, *Race and Borough Politics*, Avebury: Gower Publishing Company, 1989, p. 16)

Many of these immigrants, hard-working and capable, began to prosper, while the level of

unemployment, low since the war, began to rise again. So further resentment was felt by the white population. By the 1970s this feeling was rising. In 1968 Enoch Powell, then a member of Edward Heath's shadow cabinet and an MP in an area where racial tension was rising, publicly proclaimed the danger of immigrants overrunning the country, and was felt to have inflamed the situation. So from the 1970s violent conflict occasionally erupted between white and various non-white youths, with the police trying to keep order in the streets. Unrest on this scale for 'ethnic' reasons was a new development in Britain.

Immigrants continued to contribute to British life and established themselves in stable jobs, particularly in the retail trade. In 1988 Julia Bush, of Nene College, Northampton, interviewed a 75 year-old Bengali. This remarkable man had come to Britain in 1937 and had lived in the Midlands for twenty-five of the intervening years. He was one who had fought in World War Two, and then moved around the world, doing various kinds of work. Eventually, as Source 38 shows, he made enough money to buy his own restaurant. He ended the interview with the words: 'I am very happy and people all know me'.

I have been living twenty-five years in Northampton. I used to work in [the South] in a hospital for ten years, a stoker's job. Then after, I came here. My brother died here. He had one son who is still in Northampton. I came with my family, my three sons. At first I worked another three years in [a local hospital]. Then I left that job and went to [a light engineering works]. I worked there sixteen months then I got some money and I started the business. You know [a local district]? There, I ran the Bombay Restaurant for two years, the first Indian Restaurant in Northampton. Then I sold it and bought another in _____ Street. Then I went back home to Bangla Desh in 1973–74. I took my son and he married. Then after in 1976 I came back again to this country. My son stayed in Bangla Desh, then he came and I went back there. I stayed three years, then came again in 1984.

Why did you decide to come back?

Why? Well, you know these girls [his daughters], they said all the time 'I want to go to London'. So we came.

Source 39 Extract, slightly adapted to minimise identification, from interview with a widely-travelled and experienced Northampton resident (included in a Resource Unit by Julia Bush entitled *Moving On: Northamptonshire and a Wider World*, Northampton, Nene College Publishers, 1990, p. 2)

Ethnic issues have to be treated with great sensitivity, especially in ethnically-mixed schools. However, most children will have experiences to contribute to the 'movements of people' issue. These two sources well illustrate one aspect of the third heading in the 1995 Order: '. . . lives of people at different levels of society in different parts of Britain', though obviously there is immense scope for material about other 'levels of society' in other places in Britain. Fortunately, there is plenty of such material if it can be located. If strictly factual data cannot be found, a sensitive use of children's or adult fiction can be substituted (see Chapter 9). Northern Ireland is obviously a different issue which would require particular sensitivity but which cannot be edited out of children's experience.

THE ERSKINE BRIDGE

As with Cwmbran, our last example is concerned with post-war planning. It is about the building of the Erskine Bridge across the River Clyde, which replaced an old chain ferry. Bridges built in post-war Britain have largely been designed to complete the road network. The Erskine Bridge is one built for this purpose in Scotland. The most important of these was the Forth Road Bridge, built alongside the famous older railway bridge, a few years earlier.

Map 3 gives some idea of where the bridge is, and suggests something about why it was built. Source 40 is an outline sketch of a bridge like the Erskine, to show how it was constructed.

After 1945 it was expected that there would be much more demand for people and goods to cross the Clyde downstream from Glasgow. One reason was that many people on the north side had been unemployed because the great shipyards around Clydebank were not building as many ships, but there was more work round Paisley, on the south side. Another reason was that the tourist industry in the Western Highlands was expected to expand, and people coming by

coach or private car from England would want to get there without having to go through Glasgow.

Twenty years later, things had changed – as at Cwmbran. The 1960s were an age of optimism when many people expected new developments in technology to be the means of building a more prosperous society. Although there was no more work on the north bank than before, on the south side there were new industries. Actually, at Erskine itself, one of Scotland's New Towns was being built. The road system in and round Glasgow had been re-planned, including the westward extension of the M8 Edinburgh–Glasgow motorway on the south side. Part of this plan was for a high-level Erskine bridge at last, with tolls to pay to help repay the cost of building the bridge, which was to be designed and built by some of the leading experts in Britain. Starting in 1967, it took four years to build. When it was due to be opened, the *Scotsman*, a national newspaper, included an article about it, part of which is reproduced in Source 41.

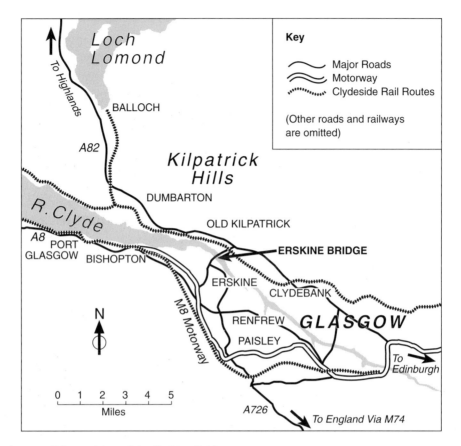

Map 3 Sketch map of the position of the Erskine Bridge

ERSKINE BRIDGE
IS BIGGEST OF ITS KIND

Erskine Bridge, with its 1000 ft long main span high over the Clyde estuary, nine miles west of Glasgow, is the biggest bridge to be opened in Scotland since the Forth road bridge was completed in 1964. With its tall, slender piers and long shallow deck curving along both approaches, Erskine is one of the most graceful bridges ever to be built.

Technically, it is described as a cable-stayed bridge and, with a single cable over each of the steel masts above the main piers, it is the biggest bridge of its kind anywhere in the world. Everywhere Erskine will be recognised as an outstanding example of British engineering design and construction, demonstrating once again the lead that British engineers have in bridge engineering . . .

Its opening to traffic today by Princess Anne will put a seal on four years of close co-operation between the Scottish Development Department, the principal designers, . . . and the many contractors and suppliers . . . who fabricated and erected the steelwork of the bridge . . .

For centuries there has been a ferry crossing of the Clyde between Old Kilpatrick and Erskine, and even as long ago as the 1930s, the growth of traffic made a bridge desirable. By the 1950s, the continued growth of traffic, and plans for the development of Clydeside, both confirmed the inadequacy of the ferry ...

With its approaches, the bridge provides an essential road link for all future developments on both sides of the Clyde that will enable industrial as well as tourist traffic to avoid the centre of Glasgow.

Source 40 Sketch of a cable-stayed bridge, similar to the Erskine Bridge

On the north side, traffic from the bridge is led on to the A82 by the Dalnottar Interchange, which also provides local connections for Old Kilpatrick.

The southern approaches comprise a mile of the new Bishopton Bypass, a three-level motorway interchange at Craigton and another mile of motorway leading through the toll area to the bridge itself. Local road connections that will have an especial value to Erskine New Town have been built in the toll area where the bridge administration building is also sited.

Source 41   Extract from *The Scotsman*, 2 July 1971

Source 41 tells something about the bridge itself and why it was built. The rest of the article from which the source was taken shows that the whole bridge, including the curved approaches, was over 4000 feet long, with a straight central span, 1000 feet long, across the Clyde itself. A 'cable-stayed' bridge (the term mentioned in the source: see Source 40) is one with towers at each end of the main span, each with cables running down at an angle on each side to support the 'deck'. At Erskine, the deck was the top part of a welded steel box girder, square in section, which ran the whole length. As with most other bridges of this sort, it had to be built from both ends with extreme accuracy, otherwise it might not have met properly in the middle. They took great care; and it did meet.

Source 41 shows that Erskine was not just a road bridge, it was much more useful than that. Source 42 also shows how all the engineers who designed and built it, and many other people in Scotland, were proud of their new bridge and had great expectations of it. So the opening of the bridge was a great occasion. It shows what sort of duty the Royal Family is expected to perform in the twentieth century, for Princess Anne was invited to open the Erskine Bridge.

Today's Royal Opening

2.50	*Presentations at the Toll Plaza.*
3.00	*Princess Anne will cut a tape to open the bridge.*
3.20	*On the Renfrew side of the centre of the bridge the Princess will unveil a plaque commemorating the opening of the bridge.*
3.25	*Crossing to the Dumbartonshire side, the Princess will unveil a plaque giving recognition to all those engaged in the building of the bridge.*
3.40	*At the North Pier the Royal Party boards the Erskine Ferry to return to the South Pier.*
3.55	*Tea in a marquee near the Toll Plaza.*
4.20	*The Princess leaves the Toll Plaza by car.*

Source 42   Extract from *The Scotsman*, 2 July 1971

We know that 2 July 1971 was a dry cloudy day and that the Princess was wearing a light lemon-coloured coat with peaked cap to match, and dark blue gloves and shoes. At exactly the right time, in the middle of the bridge, she cut the tape, surrounded by officials, and with workers in the background behind a 'cordon' of police.

Since 1971, there have been further changes:

- It had been expected that people from the north side would go to work on the south side, but there was not enough work there.
- Especially with the growth of package holidays, many of the people from England who might have taken their holidays in the Highlands of Scotland went instead to Spain and other countries in the sun. (We have seen how package holidays also affected Billy Butlin's camps.)
- It had been expected that some people living on the north side would cross the bridge and drive along the M8 into Glasgow, but they found it easier to go straight along the A82, or to use the newly-electrified railway with its subsidised fares into the city centre. So this splendid new bridge has not fulfilled all the expectations of the people who had it built. It

has carried much less traffic than, for example, the Forth Road Bridge mentioned earlier. Recently, however, the tolls have shown that traffic is now increasing: and of course the Erskine Bridge has been very useful as a carrier of all those pipes and cables.

SUGGESTED ACTIVITIES

The two sources allow several possibilities for use with children:

- From Source 41, work out, with the class, why the bridge was built and what difference it was expected to make.
- Using Source 42, write a description of Princess Anne's visit on 2 July 1971. Say why she went; how long she was at the Erskine Bridge; think why the Royal Party was taken on the old Erskine Ferry; and guess how the Princess travelled to Scotland and back. How much of her day did it probably take?
- Describe the bridge itself. This would be particularly useful if it were related to work in Design Technology on bridges, showing the difference between 'cable-stayed' bridges and other kinds of bridge such as:

  arch bridges (pack-horse bridges, or the Grosvenor Bridge in Chester, once the longest in the world), or the first-ever iron bridge which gives Ironbridge, in Telford, its name;
  beam bridges (the flat sort which carry railways over roads almost everywhere);
  suspension bridges (Clifton, Severn, Humber, or the Forth Road Bridge already mentioned);
  cantilever bridges (the Forth Rail Bridge);
  tubular bridges (the rail bridge at Conwy in North Wales);

  tied-arch bridges such as the one at Runcorn, or one of the three across the Tyne in Newcastle.
    There are useful books such as Andrew Dunn's *Structures: Bridges* and Neil Ardley's *How We Build Bridges* (see Bibliography).

- If children are interested and construction materials are available, they could make a simple model of a cable-stayed bridge, based on Source 40.
- Starting with Map 3 they could make individual maps, or a big class map, to show the location of the Erskine Bridge. This could be linked with work on rivers in geography.
- They could make a list of the bridges near home, and say what kind they are, and when they were built. If they can find out who opened one of them, they could make up a likely time-table for the opening ceremony.
- They could make a map showing what new road links have been built in their own area since 1945, and say what was expected of them. Has it worked out that way?

If any of the children have actually been across the Erskine Bridge, or have even seen it, their contribution would obviously be very valuable. If not, they will almost certainly know some of the other famous bridges. In such ways History can be linked with Geography and Design Technology.

CONCLUSION

These very different kinds of topics represent only a fraction of what is suggested in the 1995 Order. They do not directly refer to the political story, nor to the economic depressions of the 1920s which lasted into the early 1930s, nor to the rather different economic problems of more recent times. Nor do they touch directly upon the development and modifications of the Welfare State since 1945, or on the partial achievement of greater equality between the sexes, or on the many issues associated with 'Europe'. All of these are general, complex matters to do with the economy and society, which very few young children could genuinely grasp.

In this chapter, the suggestions for work with children are unlike those made for most of the earlier sources in the book, but that is because recent history fits differently into the curriculum. For example, as we have seen, it is virtually impossible to consider them without looking at their relation to geography and technology.

The richness of the recent past is accessible in many other written sources and in a wealth of personal experience. Some further light may be shed, as already hinted in the discussion of immigration, by judicious use of historical fiction (Chapter 9). The difficulty is, of course, that of giving any kind of balanced picture of this complex age. At Key Stage 2, that is not a serious problem. The important aim must be to develop further the historical sense first cultivated in Key Stage 1, and to extend the practice of the five Key Elements. In this way the children can become more fully aware that these things really happened, not long ago; that things have changed even since then; and that this matters. That realisation is essential to the more systematic studies to be undertaken in Key Stage 3, and for some, it is hoped, long afterwards.

Recent Adult Fiction

Chapter 9 indicates the value of *children's* literature as an enrichment of their knowledge of Britain Since 1930. But, as with Victorian Britain, it is also valuable for primary teachers to draw on their own reading of recent *adult fiction* as a pleasurable way of deepening their own understanding of this most recent past. So great is the scope of such written sources that it would be invidious, and virtually impossible, to select any individual authors or titles as particularly suitable for this purpose.

Yet it is possible to suggest a principle by which suitability can be assessed. The books to choose should be those which, while telling a good story, also try to portray an age: the 1930s, or World War Two or the 1960s, accurately, broadly, and without bias. On the other hand there are two sorts of literature to be treated with suspicion. One sort just uses, adapts, or distorts a period to provide the author's choice of backcloth for romance or heroism. The other presents only those aspects of an age which support a writer's particular social, political or psychological argument, bias or interpretation. Fortunately, there are plenty of the suitable sort in most libraries and, with a little practice, these can be identified, to the benefit of teachers and children alike.

Local history

Most primary curricula make some provision for local history. The first English Order, in 1991, classified it as a Supplementary Study. One unit of local history had to figure somewhere within the total eight units required; two could be included if a school so chose. The 1995 Order has retained local history as a compulsory part of the Key Stage 2 curriculum, but has confined the local study to one topic. This invites some liaison with local geography which is also obligatory, but permits considerable choice of material. The flexibility allowed by the 1995 Order in interpreting 'long', 'short' and 'local' gives individual schools considerable scope to tailor their work to their particular requirements. For example, in the choice between 'Victorian Britain' and 'Britain Since 1930', too, it might be possible to aim for the best of both worlds by deciding to develop a Victorian-age long-period local study and also to opt for 'Britain Since 1930'. Again, the breadth of this approach will, hopefully, suggest how the accumulated outcome of previous excellent local-studies work in primary schools over the past twenty years can be built on again.

So the local-history element in the Key Stage 2 curriculum is about freedom of choice rather than tight prescription. The sources chosen in this chapter are examples of material less readily available to schools than directories or census returns, and are intended to suggest further possibilities. They represent each kind of local material, though each school can choose only one of them.

The first, classified under 'a' in the 1995 Order, is concerned with a 'long period', the years 1700–1850 in the textile industry, and this may be welcomed by teachers whose own specialist knowledge is about the early Industrial Revolution otherwise omitted at Key Stage 2. The second example, under 'b' in the Order, does much the same for another period omitted, namely the seventeenth century, and is acceptable so long as it is linked to a national event or covers a short period of time. This includes both. The third, under 'c', illustrates a period considered in Chapter 5. All three can help to bring to life social situations which most children can easily understand. That is one of the main reasons for introducing young children to history by way of local studies.

TYPE A   ASPECT OF A LOCAL COMMUNITY OVER A LONG PERIOD OF TIME

The Textile industry in Lancashire, 1700–1850

The big changes in the textile industries which took place all over the industrial north should be borne in mind. Our sources refer only to one location: Helmshore and the Rossendale Valley, but it is by selecting a particular mill and family of employers that the general changes in the industry can be brought to life for junior children. The Turner family of Helmshore has been selected here, owing to the pioneering work by Nick Dunnachie and Helmshore Textile

Museum (see the Bibliography); but a similar approach could be based on Quarry Bank Mill, Styal, Cheshire (see *Victorian Britain* by R. Rees and J. Witherly), or on Titus Salt's mill and model village at Saltaire, near Bradford.

Originally, the woollen industry was conducted in cottage homes. Relics of this 'domestic industry' are still to be seen in the long upstairs windows of many Pennine stone cottages, which shed more light on the work within. One great advantage of this domestic industry was that the whole family was engaged. So a large family was an important economic necessity, especially when childbirth was risky and many children died young from infectious diseases. Women and children often undertook the carding (drawing out the sheep's fleece into parallel threads) and spinning of the carded wool into yarn, while the men worked the heavy treadle-driven looms on which the cloth was woven. The cloth was then taken to clothiers' houses in towns, by 'chapmen' on pack-horses: the roads were too rutted and muddy for carts. There the final processes – fulling to remove the grease, dyeing and finishing – were completed. The clothiers covered extensive areas of the country to find suitable markets for their different kinds of cloth.

In the eighteenth century, these methods of manufacture were transferred partly to cotton, imported from the East and later from America. Domestic workers were not used to cotton, but cotton thread was stronger than woollen thread. Then a series of new inventions took place, to speed up production; the flying shuttle, the carding machine, the spinning jenny, the water frame and finally the power loom. The result was that it was cotton cloth which was increasingly made and exported. Gradually, industry gravitated into the new factories such as Helmshore Mills, with their machines driven by water power from rapid streams fed by abundant rainfall. This movement was not without hardship and riots, when first the hand-spinners and then the hand-loom weavers found themselves

deprived of work. This was especially so when the demand for military equipment ended after the defeat of Napoleon. Machines were destroyed and strikes organised (in the Luddite Riots, c.1811–16).

In Source 43 Samuel Bamford gives a vivid picture of himself as a boy working side-by-side with his aunt in their home. He describes the boredom of his work, looking after the bobbin wheel (on which the spun yarn was threaded) and the rebukes he received from his aunt. (Source 22 in Chapter 6 comes from another book written by Samuel Bamford a little earlier.)

Whilst my life at the bobbin-wheel was wretched on account of the confinement, my poor old aunt had generally a sad time with me. It was scarcely to be expected that a tall, straight, round-limbed young ruffian like myself, with bare legs and feet, bare neck and a head equally denuded, save be a crop of thick coarse hair, should sit day by day twirling a wheel and guiding a thread; his long limbs cramped and doubled under a low wooden stool.

. . . I accordingly at times from a sheer inability to sit still, played all kinds of pranks, and threw myself into all kinds of attitudes, keeping my wheel going the while, lest my aunt should have it to say I was playing and neglecting my task. I generally sat near her at her work, and I must confess that I sometimes exhibited these antics from a wish to provoke rather than amuse my observant and somewhat irritable overseer. On these occasions I frequently got a rap on the head from a weaver's rod which my aunt would have beside her, whereupon I would move out of her reach and continue 'marlockin' [frolicking, or fooling about] until I got either more correction, or was dispatched on an errand, or banished into the 'loom-house' amongst the weavers.

Source 43 Extract from Samuel Bamford's autobiography *Early Days*, 1848 (reproduced in file: Nick Dunnachie, *The Turners: Merchants and Manufacturers of Helmshore*, Lancashire County Museum Service, n.d., p. 5)

RULES

TO BE OBSERVED IN THE

POWER-LOOM

Manufactory,

OF

W. & R. Turner, Helmshore.

WITH

A List of FINES attendant on neglect thereof

APRIL 1836.

	S.	D.
Any *Weaver or Spinner* being absent Five Minutes after the Bell Rings,	0	3
If absent more than Five Minutes, or entering the Room before the Bell Rings,	1	0
Any *Weaver or Spinner* allowing Ends or Pullings to lay upon the floor,	0	3
Any *Weaver or Spinner* allowing Bobbins to lay upon the Floor, or otherwise than in Skip or Jenny,	0	3
Any *Weaver* mixing the Warp Ends with the Weft Pullings,	0	2
Any *Weaver* taking away the Weft of another,	0	3
Any *Weaver* taking or exchanging Shuttles,	0	3
Any *Weaver* mixing empty Bobbins with full ones,	0	2
Any *Weavers* quarreling, each	1	0
Any *Weavers* fighting or striking each other, each	1	0
Any *Weaver or Spinner* leaving the Room between Bell Hours, except by leave,	1	0
Any *Weaver* after having downed or finished his or her Piece, neglecting to put in all the Pullings and rolling them up (Warp and Weft separate) in his or her Piece	0	6
Any Weaver leaving his or her Loom and going to that of another,	0	3
Any Weaver neglecting to weave up his or her Bobbins (*except when they cannot be done, and the fault is in the Spinning, and in that case to be determined by the Overlooker) per Bobbin,*		
If the fault is in the Spinning, the Spinner to forfeit for every such Bobbin or attempt his or her Loom or Looms.		

Source 44   Rules for workers at Helmshore Weaving Mill (from Nick Dunnachie, *The Turners: Merchants and Manufacturers of Helmshore,* Lancashire County Council Museum Service)

The Turner family bought land at Helmshore, near Haslingden, in 1789, and built a mill combining woollen and cotton manufacturing. Two generations later, one of the family, William Turner, introduced a huge 'overshot' water wheel (driven by water cascading down from above), much as Samuel Greg did at Quarry Bank. William Turner had an innovative mind and eventually became one of the most successful mill-owners in the country. He kept firm control of his 'operatives' (workers) through his Mill Manager and Overlookers in charge of each workroom.

The Rules of 1836 in Source 44 kept the workers under control by fines; one shilling for a weaver not finishing his/her 'piece' correctly was worth about half a day's wages. It is noticeable that these were negative rules, fining workers for mistakes, compared with the more positive rules at Sevington School (Source 28). The second rule is rather confusing in that a worker was fined one shilling for coming late and also for coming early! It may be that William Turner did not want workers to stand about in groups stirring up opposition to management. Overlookers controlled workers with military precision and used a whip when they thought it necessary.

But, at that time, William Turner would have been considered a benevolent employer, outside the workroom at least. He looked after the housing, health and education of his workforce and employed some workers in their own homes for, as we have seen, the transition from domestic to factory work was a gradual one. He also brought unemployed agricultural workers from Suffolk, transporting them by wagon and canal and again wagon by way of London and Manchester. In Source 45 it is interesting to notice that Turner paid the migrants the same wage as other workers.

He also became a powerful leader of employers in the Rossendale valley; he built a church, and a school, acted as a JP, gave money to build a turnpike road and eventually a railway (East Lancs. Railway) which ran past his mill, for better distribution of his cotton cloth. (Part of the East Lancs. Railway is a steam railway now.) In conformity with contemporary assumptions, he had a poor view of female capability, for his will directed that if he had no sons, his property should be sold at his death: in fact, his wife and eight out of eleven daughters outlived him!

Turner was one of the manufacturers who made most use of the government migration scheme of 1835–37, by which unemployed agricultural workers from the south of England were brought to industrial villages in the north, where labour was scarce. Some ten families with a total of 96 persons came to Helmshore, mostly from Suffolk. The migrants went by wagon to Paddington, London, basin of the Grand Junction Canal where they were put aboard a Pickford's boat and taken without further charge to Manchester, a voyage of five days. At Helmshore the migrants were housed at Tan Pits. It might be supposed that Turner used the scheme to recruit cheap labour, but this is probably untrue. Details of the wages Turner agreed to pay the migrants and the wages he was paying at the same time to his power-loom weavers have been recorded in Parliamentary papers. The migrants were to receive 10/- a week for the first year, 11/- a week for the second and 12/- a week for the third. Power-loom weavers were being paid 10/- a week if aged between 12 and 18 and 11/- a week if aged above 18. One of the migrants, a joiner, started at 15/- a week with two yearly increments of 1/- a week to follow.

Source 45   Extract from *The Helmshore Historian*, 1961 (reproduced in file: Nick Dunnachie, *The Turners: Merchants and Manufacturers of Helmshore*, Lancashire County Museum Service, n.d., p. 18)

SUGGESTED ACTIVITIES

This topic can be approached with children through activities such as visits, work on local records and books, and role-playing where appropriate. In this case, imaginative work can be suggested by the sources:

- Samuel Bamford irritating his aunt by his 'marlockin', written from his aunt's point of view

- a Suffolk farm 'hand' travelling to Helmshore for the first and only time in his life (by which route?): his view of the journey and of Helmshore
- a discussion between two leading workers obeying or disobeying the 1836 Rules
- William Turner discussing his will with his solicitor

Some children may want to find out more about how the machines worked from more technical books such as the recent very useful one already mentioned on p. 80 – *Victorian Britain*. Others may want to make a map showing which markets the Helmshore clothiers patronised. Similar approaches would be suitable for other local topics, such as examples of the beginnings of industrial development in other areas, provided that local museum and archive material is suitable and readily available for schools, as nowadays it often is. Such work could be closely linked to 'Victorian Britain' – or referred back to, if that period is to be studied in a subsequent year.

TYPE B   LOCAL COMMUNITY'S INVOLVEMENT IN A PARTICULAR EVENT

Charles II's escape after the Battle of Worcester 1651

The Civil War allows children to encounter the seventeenth century which follows on well from the Tudors.

Charles, son of the executed King Charles I, came to England from France to reclaim his father's crown but was defeated by Oliver Cromwell, the future Lord Protector, at Worcester in 1651. His escape to France after one and a half months' evading Cromwell's soldiers is one of the most courageous and daring escapades in English history. Nearly thirty years later, he dictated his adventures to Samuel Pepys, the diarist (see Sources 2 and 5 in Chapter 3 and also Chapter 2, p. 17). Pepys wrote in shorthand and in code, and this account was the first of his manuscripts to be deciphered, before an attempt was made to do the same for the famous diary itself.

At first, Charles wanted to flee north from Worcester to Scotland, as the Scots had sent him a contingent of soldiery at Worcester (see Map 4). This proved too difficult, and so did an attempt to cross the River Severn in to Wales, so he turned back with some Royalist supporters and decided to head south for a Welsh port or for Bristol and to sail for France from there. At one stage he also thought of making for London. By now he was on foot, disguised as a country farmer, with just one supporter (see Source 46).

This made me take the resolution of putting myself into a disguise, and endeavouring to get afoot to London, in a country-fellow's habit, with a pair of ordinary grey-cloth breeches, a learthern [sic] doublet, and a green jerkin, which I took [found] in the house of White Ladys. I also cut my hair very short, and flung my cloathes into a privy-house [lavatory], that nobody might see that anybody had been stripping themselves.

He [Major Careless] told me, that it would be very dangerous for me either to stay in that house, or to go into the wood, there being a great wood hard by Boscobel, that he knew but one way how to pass the next day, and that was, to get up into a great oak, in a pretty plain place, where we might see round about us; for the enemy would certainly search at the wood for people that had made their escape. Of which proposition of his I approving, we (that is to say, Careless and I) went, and carried up with us some victuals for the whole day, viz. bread, cheese small bear [sic], and nothing else, and got up into a great oak, that had been lopt some three or four years before, and being grown out again, very bushy and thick, could not be seen through, and here we staid all the day.

Source 46   Extracts from *King Charles Preserved: an Account of his Escape after the Battle of Worcester, dictated by the King himself to* SAMUEL PEPYS (Miniature Books, the Rodale Press, 1956, pp. 10, 18–19)

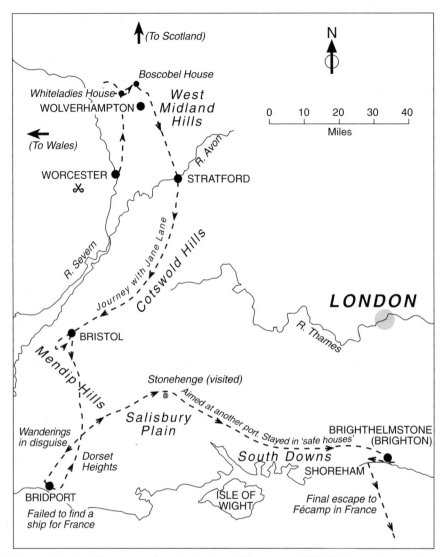

Map 4 Sketch Map of Charles II's escape after the Battle of Worcester, 1651. We know from various written sources that this was the way he went. He kept to higher ground when he could, to avoid forests and marshes, and when on main roads he took his chance. He travelled with other loyal companions after he left Jane Lane. On the way, he had several more narrow escapes

First, he was obliged to hide in the houses of the few local Royalist supporters: White Ladies' House and Boscobel House, not far from Wolverhampton. It was in the grounds of Boscobel House that he came nearest to being captured when he hid in the branches of an oak tree. The second paragraph of Source 46 conveys his recollection of that episode. Eventually he rode on horseback, calling himself Will Jackson, the servant of Jane Lane from Boscobel House, to

visit a relative of hers at a house near Bristol. 'Will' rode with Jane side-saddle in front of him. He thereafter had many other adventures, with other companions drawn from local Royalists (in those days the 'local communities' were mostly divided, often bitterly, between Royalists and Parliamentarians). Eventually he reached Shoreham in Sussex, not far from Brighton, and there just managed to embark for France.

This story may be looked upon as an event in

the local history of the three main localities and regions in which the drama took place: the West Midlands, the Bristol area and the Sussex coast. In this way an important royal figure can link local study to an important national event. Consultation with local libraries and record offices could furnish more detail about this event from other books and documents.

Both these sources, preferably supplemented from libraries and records and also by Map 4, could be used for discussion led by a teacher, for imaginative illustrative work, mapwork and role-play. A modern Ordnance Survey map would provide a sharp contrast with the seventeenth-century landscape traversed by the fugitive prince. Schools in the key areas could perhaps undertake field work, particularly by visiting Boscobel House (English Heritage).

On a broader front, study of Charles' flight could lead into a general consideration of life in the mid-seventeenth century, as a background to work on the Civil War. For the years 1649 to 1660 witnessed England's one experiment in dispensing with a monarchy. As younger children hear discussion about the future of the present-day Royal Family, they can come to see how history can throw light on events to-day while learning that the present never actually reproduces the past. They can also come to think about the 'success' and 'failure' of the Commonwealth experiment and to appreciate, through the hardships of Charles' flight, his determination after his restoration 'never to go on his travels again'.

The Civil War itself suggests other possibilities for local topics with national significance, such as the Battle of Marston Moor (1644) near York, or the Siege of Lathom House, not far from Southport (1648). The 1995 Order suggests some other local examples from other periods of English history. One such topic might be the 'Peterloo Massacre' which occupied just one fateful day in Manchester in 1819. On that occasion, 16 August, a large crowd of people from the Manchester area came together in St Peter's Square to hear Henry Hunt ('Orator Hunt') speak about the need to extend the suffrage (vote) to more people, especially working people. A riot broke out when the Manchester Yeomanry on horseback tried to break up the meeting, and eleven people were killed. This incident was nationally important, as a step towards the reform of Parliament during the nineteenth century. (The event itself acquired its familiar title from St Peter's Square and from its occurrence four years after the Battle of Waterloo.)

In fact, most localities and regions have their own 'celebrity events', some more conspicuously important than others. In any one place, judgment has to be exercised as to whether their choice of local event merits inclusion as being of national importance, rather than being trivial or otherwise unsuitable. Each worthwhile event virtually suggests its own approaches for children. Each school has to devise its own way of handling those approaches, and of considering whatever place within their reach has, at least once, played its part in the national story.

TYPE C   LOCAL ILLUSTRATION OF A PERIOD TAUGHT AS A MAIN TOPIC

Tudor Chester

This topic illustrates the third type of local history suggested in the 1995 Order. It relates to 'Life in Tudor Times', and in particular to Henry VIII's dissolution of the monasteries and to 'ways of life in a town'. It could be studied along with such work, and could be the basis for a visit to Chester for schools within reach. The city today has few visible signs of Tudor life in its buildings, because most of the sixteenth-century houses were made of wood and plaster and have been replaced by nineteenth-century brick or stone, though some of them have been painted in imitation 'black-and-white'.

To understand the two original sources, some knowledge of the Tudor city's economic and social life is needed. This was the age when Guilds developed in importance in different trades. Some of these Guilds became very prosperous and traded far afield. Leather-workers, shoemakers (cordwainers) and glovers were the most prosperous. These Guilds accepted 'indentured' apprentices from other areas. An *indenture* was a legal agreement between a parent or guardian and a master craftsman, binding a young person to serve as his apprentice under tuition for a period of time, usually seven years. In return board and lodging was provided. After 'serving time', the apprentice was entitled to earn a wage. Later, after making a 'masterpiece', he could himself become a master. The agreement, once made, was divided in two, one part for each party. If there was any argument, the two parts could be fitted together, like teeth: hence the term 'in*dent*ure'.

The Guilds also encouraged the Mystery Plays, instituted in earlier centuries. These plays, now revived, were taken round the city in procession on carts. Even when these plays died out, later in the century, the Midsummer Show was retained. Horse-racing on the Roodee, in a bend of the River Dee, also became popular.

But Tudor Chester also had its full share of unemployment, plague, sweating sickness and devastating fires. Punishments meted out for wrong-doing included the stocks, whipping, and for the most serious crimes, the gallows.

During the sixteenth century, Chester changed in other ways too. Henry VIII dissolved St Werburgh's Abbey and many other religious houses in about 1540, but the present cathedral, also dedicated to St Werburgh, was founded, and Chester became the centre of a diocese in the newly-established Church of England. Since the River Dee had not then begun to silt up, Chester was a major port for the growing coastwise trade and for commerce with Ireland, while it also became one of the principal gateways into nearby Wales, newly united with England (the Tudor monarchs were themselves a Welsh family). So,

from being a small country town inside the remains of its Roman walls, Tudor Chester emerged as one of England's major regional centres, much more important then than either Liverpool or Manchester, and with distinctive characteristics of its own.

One of these was, and still is, the *Rows*, consisting of covered shops on two levels, whose origins puzzled travellers. The first of the Chester sources is Source 47 and was by William Smith, in a topographical account written late in the reign of Elizabeth I but not published until the next century.

The Buildings of the City are very ancient; and the Houses builded in such sort, that a man may go dry, from one place of the city to another, and never come in the street; but go as it were in Galleries, which they call, The Roes, *which have Shops on both sides, and underneath, with divers fair staires to go up or down into the street. Which manner of building, I have not heard of in any place of Christendome ... It is a goodly sight to see the number of fair Shops, that are in these Rowes, of Mercers, Grocers, Drapers and Haberdashers, especially in the street called,* The Mercers Row. *Which street, with the Bridge street (being all one street) reacheth from the High Crosse to the Bridge, in length 380 paces of Geometry, which is above a quarter of a mile.*

Source 47   Description by William Smith of the Rows in Chester, written in Elizabeth I's reign and published later in Daniel King, *Vale Royall of England* [part 1], 1656 (quoted in B. E. Harris in 'The Debate on the Rows', *Journal of Chester Archaeological Society*, 67, 1984, p. 8). The 'debate' was about why the Rows were built that way; for example, was it for defence, or a continuation of a Roman style after the end of the Roman occupation?

Source 47 could be used before a visit to Chester by local schools. Chester City Council has published a reasonably-priced guide, *The Unique Chester Rows* which includes detailed information about the buildings on the Rows, with a map. Laminated copies of the map may be bought for classroom use. Pairs of children could study a

---

In the shope [shop]

Item a port mantue [portmanteau: bag]	xijd	[12d]
Item a chere [chair]	ijs	[2s]
Item 2 owlld goulden quyshenes [cushions]	xijd	
Item 2 owlld pesses [pieces] of Irone and a peare of tonnges [pair of tongs]	xvid	[16d]
Item 3 paryinge Irones (i.e. irons with which to pare material, presumably leather)	xvid	
Item a peare of sheres to cute plat with (a 'plat' may have been a sheet of leather)	xijd	
Item a beme [?] knyffe a noulld [an old] sythe an ansill [anvil?]	ijs	
Item 6 pesses of whyt kerse[y] (a coarsecloth) that lyeth (?) to pawne for	viii li	[£8]

In John Houghtones shope

Item a prese [press: chest]	vjs	[6s]
Item a coffer [cupboard: chest]	iijs iiijd	[3s. 4d]
Item 2 shillfes [shelves]	viijd	[8d]
Item a chere and a quyshene	xijd	
Item 2 gelues [gallows: braces], 2 shackeles a Racke a peare of hornes a wave (?) a chysst [chest]	xd	[10d]

Source 48 Extract from the Probate Inventory for Robert Brerewood, 1601, by courtesy of Cheshire County Record Office, who also advised about the transcription
NOTE
The modern words and (pre-decimal) coinage are given in square brackets the first time they appear. Square brackets also indicate where modern words have an extra letter. Round brackets indicate explanations.

Where it is not clear what a word is or means, this is shown by a question mark. Some words may be archaic terms used in the glovers' trade. As the original document shows, the words are not only in sixteenth-century writing, but not always clear, so there has to be a little guesswork.

As regards numbers, the final 'one' is always a 'j'.

'Item' is the Latin for 'also': that is where the modern word 'item' comes from.

small part of the Rows, which dominate the four main streets, and could work out how different each part would have looked in the sixteenth century when compared with today.

Source 48 is from the 1601 inventory of an important Guildsman, Robert Brerewood, and gives details of the items in his shop when he died. An *inventory* is a list of goods found in a person's possession after he or she died. (In Latin, *invenire* means 'to find'.) This one also includes items in the shop that Robert Brerewood had rented out to John Houghton, a clerk at St Mary's who kept Robert's account books in order. A reduced copy of the original, a rather poorly written and faded document, is reproduced as Source 49. (Some inventories are easier to read, see Appendix p. 118.)

As a wealthy glover (glovemaker), Robert Brerewood played a leading part in Chester life. A recent historian, D. M. Woodward, has stated that Robert 'stood head and shoulders above his fellow craftsmen, as he did in all things'. He was not only a glover, but also a shoemaker, farmer and timber merchant. He became a freeman of the city, mayor and sheriff. Although he remained illiterate and could only make his mark (x) on his will, he left £1600 in property and money when he died, and that made him quite a wealthy man in late Tudor times.

Source 49 Copy of extract from Probate Inventory of Robert Brerewood, Chester merchant, transcribed in Source 48

SUGGESTED ACTIVITIES

This part of the inventory for his 'shoppe' and John Houghton's, name the tools used for making leather gloves and shoes. Both shops had a chair and cushion, which shows that furniture was not upholstered. Activities might include:

- The values of all the items could be added up to find out the total value of the two shops
- Both sources could form part of an account of Tudor Chester

As an alternative, children could be led to imagine life in the sixteenth century as seen by

- Robert, John, or one of Robert's apprentices
- another shop owner on the Rows
- a canon (clergyman) attached to the new cathedral
- an actor in the Mystery Plays

Ideally, for this purpose, these two original sources would need to be supplemented by other documents and books to be found in the two record offices in Chester (City and County) and in the local collection in the Chester Library. It would be interesting to compare Robert Brerewood's inventory with that of John Garards, a pauper (1715) in the Appendix, p. 118.

Other cities and towns with significant remains and records of Tudor times could be similarly incorporated into a local history topic, with adaptations to circumstances. In any such study, fieldwork must play an important part, but it is obviously important to design the preparation of that fieldwork thoroughly and systematically, so that a visit becomes much more than the 'day out'. With careful foresight, a visit can be designed so that it is fairly weather-proof – a consideration which, as William Smith would have been pleased to point out, causes less of a problem in the Rows of Chester.

Monumental brasses, stone tablets and glass windows are examples of other local sources which often include words. But that wording, whether in Latin, Norman-French or period English, is sometimes difficult to read. So no examples are given in this book. However, in any locality it is worthwhile to look at churches and other public buildings and to consult the local history section of a public library to find out what children may be able to 'rub', photograph or copy (with permission) and interpret.

Historical fiction

DEFINING TERMS

The term 'historical fiction' needs clarifying. The Schools Council defined this literary form as 'stories seriously intended to recreate historical situations'. This definition makes it seem like an ideal written source for children, but both historians and linguists have expressed concern about using historical fiction in this way. Some historians see History as a science which has no room for narrative containing ideas about which there is no known evidence. Literature specialists are worried about dissecting a story to extract its historical content and so destroy the reader's ability to enjoy the literature for its own sake. Perhaps the final word should go to an American author (Freedman, 1992) writing on the use of non-fiction texts and suggests that 'fact and fiction are different truths. Fiction is fact's elder sister'.

In this chapter we will set out a rationale for using historical fiction as an important historical written source and suggest ways in which it can be used effectively with primary children. A Bibliography entry for each title mentioned in this chapter can be found at the end of the book. The chapter will not include period fiction which is categorised as documentary source material for the time in which it was written. The term period fiction is generally used to cover children's literature written in the Victorian or Edwardian era which contains language and settings which may be unfamiliar for today's children; for example *The Railway Children* by E. Nesbitt and *The Secret Garden* by Frances Hodgson Burnett.

Period fiction for children can also include extracts from adult novels by writers such as Dickens and Kingsley. Close inspection of such texts can produce some good insights into social and domestic conditions in Victorian and Edwardian times. The chart on p. 90 highlights the value of good historical fiction.

Guidelines for evaluating historical fiction

Historical fiction must meet the demands of good writing, but it has special criteria beyond this.

- Does it work as a good story?
- Has fact and fiction been well blended so that it does not read as a devious attempt to cover historical information?
- Is the story as accurate and authentic as possible?
- Is the language appropriate to the times?
- Does the dialogue convey a feeling of period without seeming artificial?
- Are background details authentic or in keeping with known information about the times?
- Is the theme relevant for the challenges of today as well as those of the past?
- Are different points of view presented?

Like all guidelines these need to be related to the age and ability of the children. Historical fiction which uses language appropriate for the times may be a more suitable criteria for older primary children.

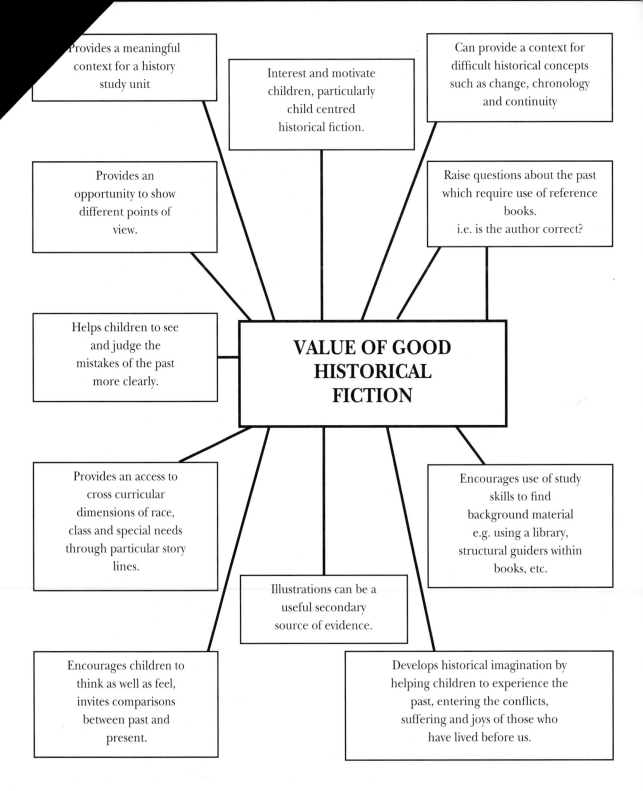

Provides a meaningful context for a history study unit

Interest and motivate children, particularly child centred historical fiction.

Can provide a context for difficult historical concepts such as change, chronology and continuity

Provides an opportunity to show different points of view.

Raise questions about the past which require use of reference books.
i.e. is the author correct?

Helps children to see and judge the mistakes of the past more clearly.

VALUE OF GOOD HISTORICAL FICTION

Provides an access to cross curricular dimensions of race, class and special needs through particular story lines.

Encourages use of study skills to find background material e.g. using a library, structural guiders within books, etc.

Illustrations can be a useful secondary source of evidence.

Encourages children to think as well as feel, invites comparisons between past and present.

Develops historical imagination by helping children to experience the past, entering the conflicts, suffering and joys of those who have lived before us.

This form of evaluation can be used initially by teachers to evaluate historical fiction books they would like to use with the class, but more able primary readers could use it as a starting point to draw up their own list of criteria as part of a literature project on historical fiction.

Categories of historical fiction

Historical fiction can be divided into three categories:

- documentary historical fiction
- researched historical fantasy
- creative history

Documentary
Historical fiction tends to deal with historical periods and people for which there is more available evidence. The story will be woven around real events and people, making extensive use of the sources of the period. Thus in *The Flither Pickers* by Theresa Tomlinson, the author has used photographs of the late Victorian era as a starting point for a story about the women who collected bait for the fishermen in Whitby. This was done as a family activity and the women received no cash payments for their work.

Researched
Historical fantasy contains a greater element of creativity. There is still an authentic historical background, but a much stronger fictional element is woven in to provide a story context with an element of fantasy. Jill Paton Walsh's *The Chance Child* does this. In the book, two children from the present move back into the past and look at different forms of child labour to reach some understanding about the ill-treated child who lives with them. The boy in the story is himself using written source material from the Victorian period to research a school project on child labour. Alison Uttley's *A Traveller in Time* moves its main character to the sixteenth century and involves her with a plot to free Mary Queen of Scots. Both these books are challenging reads

and are probably more suitable for reading aloud by the teacher.

Creative
Historical fiction involves people and places in the far more distant past. As less original evidence is available there are greater gaps in our knowledge of events and life at that time. The author fills these gaps in a way that is creative rather than fantastic so that the historical information given is consistent with current knowledge and research. It is the category in which some of the most well-known children's novelists have chosen to write. Rosemary Sutcliffe must be the prime example here, with her stories of Roman and Celtic Britain such as *Song for a Dark Queen* and *Eagle of the Ninth*. As with researched historical fantasy many of these titles are challenging for primary pupils and benefit from being read aloud or listened to on tape.

Costume drama
An extension of creative historical fiction, where the author creates a story set rather vaguely in the past. Little or no research has been done into the period and the story could take place almost anywhere or at any time. It may be a good read but its use for History is limited.

Picture books

The picture story book conveys its messages through two media – the art of illustrating and the art of writing. 'In a well-designed book in which the total format reflects the meaning of the story, both the illustration and text must bear the burden of narrative' (Huck *et al*, 1995). This differs from an illustrated book where no attempt is made to tell the whole story. A good picture book conveys its meaning in both the art and the text.

Some picture books can be put into the category of historical fiction and although they are particularly suitable for early years pupils they can also be used with older pupils. The two models on pages 92 and 93 show how

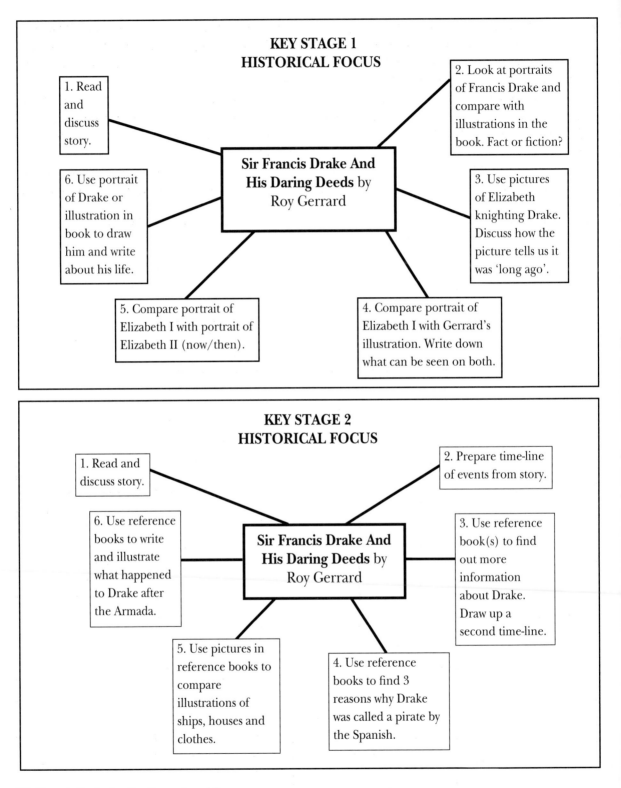

KEY STAGE 1
HISTORICAL FOCUS

1. Read and discuss story.

2. Look at portraits of Francis Drake and compare with illustrations in the book. Fact or fiction?

Sir Francis Drake And His Daring Deeds by Roy Gerrard

6. Use portrait of Drake or illustration in book to draw him and write about his life.

3. Use pictures of Elizabeth knighting Drake. Discuss how the picture tells us it was 'long ago'.

5. Compare portrait of Elizabeth I with portrait of Elizabeth II (now/then).

4. Compare portrait of Elizabeth I with Gerrard's illustration. Write down what can be seen on both.

KEY STAGE 2
HISTORICAL FOCUS

1. Read and discuss story.

2. Prepare time-line of events from story.

Sir Francis Drake And His Daring Deeds by Roy Gerrard

6. Use reference books to write and illustrate what happened to Drake after the Armada.

3. Use reference book(s) to find out more information about Drake. Draw up a second time-line.

5. Use pictures in reference books to compare illustrations of ships, houses and clothes.

4. Use reference books to find 3 reasons why Drake was called a pirate by the Spanish.

Sir Francis Drake for Key Stages 1 and 2

Roy Gerrard's *Sir Francis Drake and His Daring Deeds* can be used for younger and older pupils.

Picture books are particularly good in helping children to see how writers write and historical fiction picture books enable children to research and use visual sources as well as written sources to provide models for children for structured narratives and descriptions.

Janet and Allan Ahlberg's *Peepo* tells the story of a soldier in the 1940s getting ready for war and leaving his family. It is probably one of the most well-known examples of this genre. The story can be used to discuss the differences and similarities between domestic life now and then. Children can work in pairs from several copies of the book on one double page spread, or use one of the larger versions in a small group. Scenes which show the kitchen, bedroom and backyard are particularly suitable. Older children can then use the same text and work with reference books and

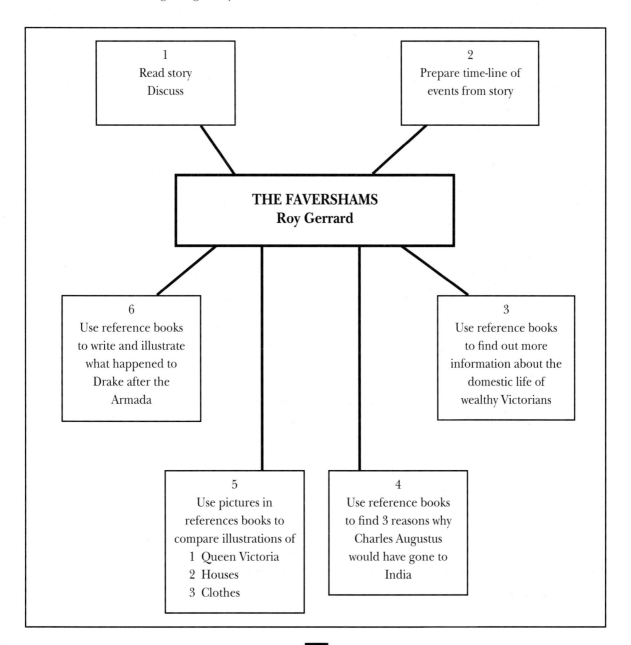

1
Read story
Discuss

2
Prepare time-line of events from story

THE FAVERSHAMS
Roy Gerrard

6
Use reference books to write and illustrate what happened to Drake after the Armada

3
Use reference books to find out more information about the domestic life of wealthy Victorians

5
Use pictures in references books to compare illustrations of
1 Queen Victoria
2 Houses
3 Clothes

4
Use reference books to find 3 reasons why Charles Augustus would have gone to India

other reference materials to find out more about the historical accuracy of the book. It may not be immediately obvious that these type of picture books are historical fiction. Illustrators like Janet Ahlberg and Sue Scullard favour historical settings, although the text itself may not relate to the historical aspects of the pictures.

Family stories such as Shirley Hughes' *Lucy and Tom's Christmas* give a narrative context for the passing of time. Other family stories such as Valerie Flournoy's *The Patchwork Quilt* illustrate how every family makes its own history by retelling family stories many times over.

Roy Gerrard is another author/illustrator who frequently chooses a historical theme. The chart on page 93 shows how one of his books on a Victorian family, *The Favershams*, can be used to develop children's research and study skills for this particular period in history. Children can do an author/illustrator study on him and make comparisons between this book and others he has written with a historical theme, such as *Sir Francis Drake* and *Matilda Jane* (about the Victorian seaside).

Using picture books to explore historical concepts

Picture books can provide a means of developing children's understanding of difficult historical concepts and can be used with pupils of any age. Books such as *Shaker Lane, The Shepherd Boy, Jack's Basket* and *Our House on the Hill* (see the Bibliography) all explore historical change over a period of time. *Our House on the Hill* and *The Shepherd Boy* are a narrative of events over the course of a year. *Jack's Basket* covers several years, while *Shaker Lane* narrates the passing of time over several decades. The stories in each of these books move forward because people, places and objects change over time. These changes are recorded as they happen and the text provides the explanation for the changing illustrations. The child is not left to make sense of the picture by themselves, as the author guides them through

the chronological change which is taking place as part of the story. The plot focuses on the changes; children can discuss the cause and effect of different changes on the story. They can record the events in the narrative on a time-line and use historical vocabulary related to the passing of time such as day, month, season and year.

A virtually wordless picture book such as Jeannie Baker's *Window* uses beautiful collage and environmental print to mark the passage of time for a boy from birth until he leaves home with his own baby. Each double page spread marks another two years. John Goodall uses a similar technique in his books recording *The Story of an English Village, The Story of a Castle, The Story of a Farm, The Story of the Seaside* and *The Great Days of a Country House*. These books follow events over hundreds of years.

The historical concept of evidence is examined in *The Sandal* by Tony Bradman and Phillipe Dupasquier. This story is of a Roman sandal and how it eventually arrives in a museum. Items in collections of local museums often have interesting stories related to them. *The Sandal* can be used to prompt children into asking how objects come into museums. Older children can research into this and make their own stories about the journeys of artefacts into museums. A link can also be made about the nature of changes in materials and an examination of the sort of objects which are less likely to decay over time.

In Mem Fox's *Wilfred Gordon McDonald Partridge*, a small boy (Wilfred Gordon) collects a series of objects which remind him about the past to show them to a very old lady to help her remember her past. The same object conjures up different memories for each of them. The story enables teachers and pupils to explore their own memories of the past and show how particular artefacts exist which provide evidence of it. Children can be asked whether they have any artefacts which have particular memories for them, a favourite teddy bear for example. These historical sources provide a means of exploring what is meant by source material, how much information it can give us about the past and how useful this information is.

HISTORICAL FICTION FOR OLDER PRIMARY PUPILS

In the following sections historical fiction books are discussed chronologically, but two other methods of using historical fiction are addressed.

1 Spiritual, moral, social and cultural dimensions

It would be possible to have a literature theme using historical fiction from different periods to examine recurring topics such as the search for freedom and the human cost of war. A literature topic like this, even focusing on one book can be seen as using curriculum content in one subject to promote pupils' spiritual, moral, social and cultural development. The sections later in this chapter sub-headed 'The world at war', 'Escape and resistance', 'Biography' and 'Movements of people' identify some books which would be useful for this.

2 Author studies

Author studies on writers such as Robert Westall and Jill Paton Walsh gave children a chance to research one creator of historical fiction in greater depth. One way of doing this is to gather together as many books by the author as possible and after reading and re-reading decide how the books are connected; think of the author's particular strengths and what ideas you want the children to discover. If one book is read aloud it provides a framework for work by the same author. A more generic literature topic on historical fiction could look at it as a specific genre and allow children to evaluate the work of several different authors. Madeleine Lindley's bookshop supply packs of historical fiction books which make such a study relatively easy to organise (contact address: Madeleine Lindley Ltd, 79 Acorn Centre, Barry Street, Oldham, OL1 3NE).

Several publishers have moved into producing historical fiction. This may be as part of a reading scheme – such as Alan Gibbons' *The Climbing Boys* in the Collins Pathways Reading Scheme, or as a special series such as Ginn History Stories for both Key Stage 1 and 2. Each of the Scholastic Study Kits covering Ancient Greece, the Anglo-Saxons and the Tudors contain a fictional story on the period by Gill Goddard. Teachers' notes accompanying the books suggest different ways in which they can be used, although those which form part of a reading scheme tend to treat the historical context as incidental. Anglia books have also produced an historical fiction series accompanied by teachers' notes. The quality varies but Anglia have been very successful at providing a written text for the average and less able reader. Barnard's *Escape from the Workhouse* for example, is an easy and rewarding read. It can be linked to work in Personal and Social Education and Religious Education about homelessness today and ways in which it is being tackled.

It is worth noting that historical fiction is not as popular as it was a generation ago as primary children who do read tend to select books about modern-day characters and settings (Huck *et al*, 1995).

Romans, Anglo-Saxons and Vikings

Rosemary Sutcliffe and Henry Treece are probably the two best-known authors who write historical fiction for children about this period. Their books do not make for easy reading, even for good readers at the top end of the primary school, but they can be adapted and read aloud, particularly if children are studying this period and can therefore bring some of their historical knowledge to an understanding of the text. The books are carefully researched and provide a good insight into many of the aspects of life in Roman Britain. Several of them have appeared on television or been broadcast on the radio, which makes them more accessible if copies of the video or audio cassette can be found.

There are several different versions of the Anglo-Saxon story of Beowulf such as Rosemary Sutcliffe's *Dragon Slayer* and Kevin Crossley-Holland's *Beowulf*. It is easy to dismiss the Beowulf story as complete fantasy for it is of a hero who killed monsters. However the story does give important historical messages as well as details about living conditions, beliefs, customs and rituals in the past. It provides considerable insight into the life of wealthy Saxons, ship burials and funerary rites as well as giving children an opportunity to study a major literature text. Similar comments could be made on other picture books showing myths and legends from other peoples studied such as the Celts, the Romans and Anglo-Saxons.

The Tudors

The Princess in the Pig Pen by J. R. Thomas, brings an Elizabethan child into the future and a strong plot gives children the opportunity to explore some of the differences and similarities between Tudor times and today. Penelope Lively's *The Ghost of Thomas Kempe* uses the same technique of bringing someone from the past into the present and using this as the focus for the plot. Deary's *A Witch in Time* moves children from the present to the past in order to solve a problem. This enables the children in the story to use some of their present-day knowledge to inform their problem-solving in the past. This particular form of historical fiction, involves transporting the main character and reader from the present day to a carefully researched past. In most of the instances the characters return to the present as wiser more

understanding people, perhaps hinting that one of the purposes of studying History is that we may learn from it.

Victorian Britain

Lady Daisy is another historical fantasy book, where a Victorian doll becomes alive in the present. The doll is found by a boy, which makes an interesting sub-plot feeding into PSE when the boy's father becomes anxious about his son's apparent interest in playing with a doll. The doll provides the boy with information for his Victorian school project. In Phillipa Pearce's *Tom's Midnight Garden* and Helen Cresswell's *The Moondial*, the child characters are transported back to a Victorian house and garden. In *Moondial* the story is based on a National Trust property which makes it particularly interesting for children who visit the property, but also provides a good starting point for children's own writing about historic buildings which they may have visited.

A class discussion on possible plots for a class book can make this a less tedious process than asking children to write their own stories after a class visit. It provides a model for future stories, particularly if children have had the opportunity to role play at the building and site. Madden's *A Teacher's Guide to Story Telling at Historic Sites*, published by English Heritage, is an example of how both English Heritage and The National Trust have seen how their buildings and sites can stimulate children's historical imagination.

Berlie Doherty's *Street Child* brings to life the story of Jim Jarvis, the orphan boy who inspired Dr Barnado to set up his homes for children in London. It has a strong story line which makes it particularly suitable for reading out aloud and can be related to RE and PSE themes. Gillian Avery's *Ellen's Birthday* is another book which comes into the category of documentary fiction as does Geoffrey Trease's *No Horn at Midnight* which takes the coming of the railways as its theme.

Britain Since 1930

A surprising number of books from this period concentrate on the war years. In some cases the plots only use the war as a starting point for the story, as in Nina Bawden's *Carrie's War* and Theresa Tomlinson's *Summer Witches*. Books like this give a great deal of information about life in the 1940s without really touching upon the horror of war. *Carrie's War* tells more about the personal wars of the living than of the war of bombs and blitzes. 'The World at War' could be a literature theme in its own right and the following section looks more closely at this. Alan Gibbons in *The Street of Tall People* looks at the rise of the fascist movement in the 1930s in London. It covers daily life in the 1930s as well as the enduring challenges presented when relationships are threatened with conflicting ideologies. *The Jaws of the Dragon* by the same author weaves a story around the Vietnamese boat people. Berlie Doherty's *Granny was a Buffer Girl* works through the emotions and experiences of three generations of one family.

'The World at War'

Few books have been written about World War One but there are many books about World War Two and the Holocaust. Several picture books might be used as an introduction with older juniors. *Rose Blanche* by Christopher Gallaz and Roberto Innocenti is the story of a girl who observes the actions of the Nazis and one day follows a van out to a concentration camp. Later she visits the camp to slip little pieces of food to the children she sees there. At the end she finds the camp empty. This would of course have been impossible, but it symbolises the efforts made by people who did resist the war in different ways. Rose Blanche was in fact the name given to a German resistance group who protested against the war.

Let the Celebrations Begin! by Margaret Wild is the story of Polish women in Belsen who were determined to make toys for the party they were going to have when the camp was liberated. The story is based on a reference to a small collection of toys found at Belsen when it was liberated. The toys were made from scraps of materials, rags and buttons. The small collection of stuffed elephants, owls and other toys makes a moving testament to the need for hope whatever the circumstances.

My Hiroshima by Junko Morimoto records in pictures and text the horror of the atomic bomb. Julia Abells' collection of photographs in *Children we remember* has a very simple linked text which tells more than anything else the horror of the Holocaust and the importance of remembering what happened.

Escape and resistance

Some of the most gripping war stories are about families who escaped to freedom or spent long periods of time hiding from the Nazis. *The Lily Cupboard* does this in a picture book format and tells the story of a Dutch couple who hid a Jewish child in a cupboard when they were visited by the Gestapo. Judith Kerr's *When Hitler Stole Pink Rabbit* is based on her own experience of escaping from Germany in the early 1930s. First she and her family went to Austria, then Switzerland and France before finally coming to England. The initial story is based in the 1930s but two further books take up the story of the difficulties of life as a Jewish refugee in wartime Britain. Although a very optimistic book, considering its subject matter, it does look at the horrendous problems which refugees have and their feeling of never really belonging anywhere.

The Upstairs Room by Johanna Reiss is another story based on the author's own experience of being hidden from the Nazis by a farm family, the Oostervelds. She and her sister spent most of their time in an upstairs room so that they would not be seen. This links in well with extracts from Anne Frank's diary and *Dear Anne Frank*, produced by Puffin, which is an anthology of writing from schoolchildren responding to the issues raised by the diary. *Ann Frank, Beyond the*

Diary is a photographic remembrance of the period with accompanying text.

Michael Morpurgo's *Waiting for Anya* tells of the dramatic rescue of French Jewish children through a village close to the Spanish frontier, and on a different theme his *Friend or Foe* tells of a child's dilemma in being helped by a German soldier and wondering whether he should help him to escape capture. *The Silver Sword* by Ian Serraillier is concerned with Polish children living and surviving by themselves during and after the war. Anne Holm's *I am David* also explores the aftermath of the war for a child who has never known any life apart from that in a prison camp.

The House of Sixty Fathers by Meindert Dejong reminds us that people in Asia also suffered during the war years. A young Chinese boy named Tien Pao and his family flee before the Japanese invasion, but are separated. Clutching his pet pig Tien Pao struggles on, not knowing where to go. He is eventually helped by a US airman and taken to a barracks where he is made the mascot of the soldiers, 'his sixty fathers'.

There are several authors who have written books about children's experiences in Britain during the bombing raids. Several of Robert Westall's books come into this category *The Machine Gunners*, *Blitz* and *A Time of Fire* are all books which draw on real life experiences to create a fictional story. Westall explains how he based *The Machine Gunners* on a newspaper report about boys in Holland finding a German plane and linked this with the events that happened when a false invasion rumour spread through Tyneside. There are parts of this book which some teachers may wish to omit; for example the boys finding the German pilot's rotting body. This does raise professional issues about whether war should be dressed up for children's consumption or be dealt with in all its enormity.

Biography

Biography often bridges the gap between historical fiction and informational books. A life story might read like fiction but like non-fiction it will be based on facts which can be documented. In the past biography written for children used more fictional techniques than those written for adults. The trend today is for more authenticity, which does make for slightly harder texts. This makes many biographies more suitable for older pupils. The checklist below drawn from Huck *et al* (1995) suggests guidelines for evaluating biography written for children.

Evaluating biography

- Choice of subject
  Is the person's life interesting and relevant for today's children?
  Will it help children to understand the past?
- Accuracy and Authenticity
  Do the text and illustrations reflect careful research?
  Are there significant omissions?
  Are there discrepancies of fact with other books?
- Style
  Is it clear and readable with background material included naturally?
- Characterisation
  Is the person presented as a believable, multi-dimensional character with both strengths and weaknesses?
- Theme
  Does the author have a fair and balanced approach?
  Does the book avoid oversimplifying the facts?

Picture book biographies

Partly in response to this difficulty, several publishers have produced picture biographies for very young children, notably Ginn, Longman and Heinemann. They have aimed them at the early years market and made some attempt to ensure that all the biographies are not just of the great and good. The challenge presented to the authors of these books is to provide a text which can be read by beginning readers. MacDonald Young Books have commissioned several well-known children's authors of historical fiction, for example Geoffrey Trease, for their series 'Historical Story Books'. These books contain more text, which allows a richer narrative to emerge. Several teachers' books on assemblies contain stories about the lives of people who have served others and this type of story can be developed at different levels once children return to their own classrooms.

Several publishers such as Puffin produce booklets and posters about authors. These are often used as a background for author studies, but could just as easily be used to examine what is meant by biography and autobiography and the links between these and historical fiction. In addition Michael Rosen's and Jill Burridge's *Treasure Islands* (Books 1 and 2) provide potted biographies and autobiographies of a number of authors. Children can also research for evidence about authors and illustrators themselves using information from book jackets and author notes inside the book.

Authors like Catherine Brighton have produced colourful picture books on Mozart and Nijinsky, which can be easily linked to work in Music and PE. These books have a much heavier text, but children could devise captions for the illustrations by the author, once they have heard the story read aloud.

The 1992 celebrations and commiserations about the arrival of Columbus in the Americas produced several books about his life and time. Jane Yolen's text for *Encounter*, beautifully illustrated by David Shannon, tells the traditional story from the perspective of a Tanio Indian boy and raises important questions about what the Spaniards did when they arrived. Jean Fritz tells a more traditional version in *The Great Adventures of Christopher Columbus*, while Postgate and Linnell in *Columbus the Triumphant Failure* trace his life story after 1492. Michael Foreman's *The Boy who sailed with Columbus* presents a very full picture of life on

the seas in 1492. A collection of these picture books on one particular man provides a good opportunity for older children to discuss the different ways in which authors have presented Columbus as well as the fact that Columbus, like us all, had several facets to his personality. It raises too the issue of making judgements on people in the past, without acknowledging the ethos of the time in which they lived. These are complex historical and literary understandings, but the use of biographical picture books enables discussion to take place based on some concrete information.

Movements of people

History has been criticised as the story of the victors. Historical fiction allows the stories of the invisible and marginalised to be told. Movement of peoples is a timeless theme. The invaders who become settlers have their story told as the victors, but the reason for their movement from one country to another can be seen as an on-going theme. Geraldine Kaye's book *A Breath of Fresh Air* looks at the Bristol slave trade and uses historical fantasy to take a child back to Bristol in the seventeenth century and sense the danger and horror of being an escaped slave. Alan Gibbons *Whose Side Are You On?* on the same theme, is based in Liverpool. In this book, time travel takes the main character back to the West Indies to look at one of the many slave rebellions which took place. The experience enables him to look again at the racist bullying taking place in his own school and inform him on the action he must take. This book also has the advantage of showing an example of struggles and victories made by slaves who did protest. Too often the history of the abolition of slavery is recounted as part of a narrative about great white men who passed laws to stop it. This story identifies another history.

A couple of picture books take up this theme as well. *Always Adam* by Oberman and Lewin looks at the movement of a Jewish family from Russia to America. It explains very clearly the reasons for their move as well as the importance of keeping their cultural identity. This is seen in terms of a prayer shawl, handed down from grandfather to grandson, both of whom are called Adam. *Tanya Moves House* by E. Abrahams tells the story of a Bangla Desh family who move from their own area which has been flooded to Britain and the fear that Tanya has about going to a new school, where she does not understand the language. In *Grandmother's Tale* by Moy McCrory, a Turkish grandmother living in Britain tells her granddaughter about what used to happen in her village when a baby was born. Like many of the picture books mentioned in this section, it brings the sadness of emigration home as well as the successes in the new land.

Historical fiction can be powerful. It is all that is left of the grand tradition of narrative writing inherited from the Victorian age, which is now so despised by academic historians. It is worth remembering that primary children are not academic historians and good historical fiction is an important way of providing an understandable context for historical knowledge.

Using historical reference books

Apart from the previous chapter on historical fiction, this book has looked at using written sources with children which come under the definition of primary source material (i.e. sources of the time). In this chapter we look at secondary source materials produced for primary children which may contain some primary source material, but which are essentially pupil texts written to help children find out more about the past.

USING NON-FICTION IN THE PRIMARY SCHOOL

Over the past few years a great deal of attention has been paid to the use of non-fiction texts in primary classrooms. There is an understanding that children cannot just be directed to the library or to a pile of books on a table and be asked to find out about the topic for themselves. They need to be taught directly both how to use the library and how to access the information. They then need support in developing a variety of different means of communicating the knowledge, skills and understandings they have made from the texts. Guiding pupils towards high-quality non-fiction takes time, but its benefits stretch across and beyond the formal curriculum.

Non-fiction

- satisfies and broadens curiosity;
- provides for depth and breadth of information and opens the way for further inquiry;
- offers accurate information and documents such accuracy;
- provides models for concise writing;
- introduces a variety of genres for both reading and writing;
- provides visuals that clarify facts;
- demonstrates the need for the logical organisation of facts;
- challenges readers to read critically;
- expands vocabulary; and
- offers options to children who prefer facts to fiction
  (adapted from Burke, E. and Glazer, S. 1994).

Using history texts

Several writers such as Mallett in *Making Facts Matter* (1992) and Neate in *Finding Out About Finding Out* (1992) have pointed out that non-fiction history texts are probably the most challenging for pupils. Work with primary pupils, in-service teachers and student teachers has identified a number of specific skills and understandings which teachers need in order to be able to help pupils 'read' texts which are aimed at the primary school market. (See the diagram on page 102.)

In this chapter it is proposed to show practical examples of ways in which teachers can help pupils learn history from pupil texts by

USING NON-FICTION TEXTS IN HISTORY TEACHING

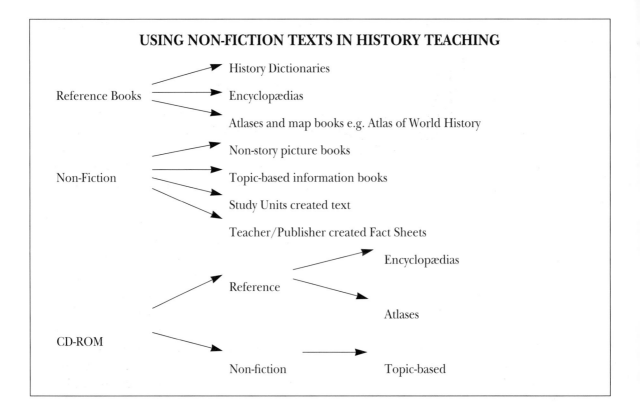

- identifying different types of non-fiction books which are useful for reference purposes in history;
- helping pupils to recognise and use structural guiders associated with these different types of non-fiction texts;
- supporting pupils in understanding the ways in which non-fiction book format works;
- developing pupils' skills in communicating their knowledge and understandings of history through producing their own written source material.

The distinction between reference books and non-fiction texts may be less obvious in a school library than in a public library, where it is generally not possible to take out reference books. Children using a set of encyclopaedias in a library will need to work in the library itself and many libraries make excellent provision for children to do this. An increasing number of schools are developing after-school facilities for children which include library provision for homework.

History dictionaries

There are still not many historical dictionaries written specifically for children, but this is a gap in the British market which is likely to be filled soon. Some of these written for adults such as Kenyon's *A Dictionary of British History*, Mills' *A Dictionary of Place-Names* and Lempriere's *Classical Dictionary* can be used quite successfully by older primary pupils.

As Mallett (1992) points out children need to acquire more than the ability to understand the alphabetical organisation of these dictionaries. They need to transfer and adapt the skills they have acquired while using a word dictionary in order to use a subject specialist dictionary. Children may like to draw up their own historical dictionary for the particular era they are studying.

This experience of authorship involves reflecting on the type of entries made in historical dictionaries as well as the need to research different aspects of the period. The work here can be linked in with the use of glossaries which are an essential part of many of the newer non-fiction pupil texts.

Encyclopaedias

Encyclopaedias may be one or many volumes and may be organised thematically or alphabetically. Most recently produced encyclopaedias are arranged alphabetically and contain an index. Using encyclopaedias for their history work means that children have an opportunity to develop research skills in context. Children should be advised about the different types of encyclopaedia which are available to them and be provided with the opportunity to explore their contents. As when using an historical dictionary they need help in developing their cross-referencing skills. If they are studying the Victorians for example, they can be encouraged to think of other possible entries such as 'Crimean' and 'Empire' which might give them further information about the Victorians. Where information is not available, the children should record the questions and identify other resources that might help, such as another encyclopaedia, non-fiction texts, atlases, wall-charts, posters, tele-text, filmstrips or videos. Public libraries, and some schools, have computerised library search facilities available and pupils can be encouraged to use these.

Often children need to ask questions about the topic so that they can think about the sort of things they need to know. The encyclopaedia may be a first stop or it may be the final source they examine.

More able readers can often cope with adult encyclopaedias which provide a great deal of information. This then requires them to develop very specific research skills in skimming and scanning, identifying and extracting main ideas, note-taking and rewriting.

Atlases and map books

Historical atlases such as Antony Mason's *The Children's Atlas of Exploration* usually combine text, illustrations and photographs with maps. Much of the children's ability to interpret historical maps will depend on their geographical skills, and because maps communicate information visually some children who have difficulty with historical text may find historical maps much more attractive and easier to use. They do have distinct problems. Historical maps often only focus on a small section of the world and because of lack of space they show just the area mentioned. Maps of the Roman Empire for example often show only the Mediterranean basin and Britain. This can be quite difficult as well as being of limited use for many primary children if they have no world map to refer to.

Primary source historical maps are sometimes contained in historical atlases for children and require very sophisticated geographical skills, as children need to have internalised the familiar world map in order to interpret the historical map.

Non-story picture books

Americans call these 'concept books' and the most common are those relating to counting and ABC books. Some of the best history non-story picture books for children are in fact produced for adults. Collections of local photographs showing 'then and now' pictures with a short caption are good examples of non-story picture books. These help to develop a historical concept – in this example that of change. Unfortunately educational publishers seem reluctant to produce similar concept books for children, although the success of books produced for the general public on old streets and buildings should encourage them to look at the potential for schools. Abell's

Children We Remember, showing pictures of children murdered during the Holocaust, is an outstanding example of the powerful message such historical concept books can provide.

Topic-based information books

These take specific topics such as transport or homes and provide a history of that particular area. Changes in the National Curriculum have meant that this thematic approach is no longer in favour with older primary pupils and books adopting a topic based approach tend to be older and less likely to contain the structural guiders required by teachers. Publishers such as Longman and Ginn in their Primary History Programmes have produced several topic history books on popular early years topics such as teddy bears, lights, streets, shops and homes. Other publishers such as Wayland, Franklin Watts and A & C Black have produced series of history topic based information books for early years pupils. These have series titles such as *History Mysteries* (Franklin Watts) and *History from Photographs* (Wayland). The readability levels in these books is often quite high, although high quality photographs mean that the visuals convey the messages.

Although publishers are producing less of these topic based information books for older pupils, they are useful because they really force children to use structural guiders such as contents pages if they want to find the information effectively. If children are studying a particular period in history, topic based information books on transport, homes or toys will provide them with relevant information, but it will need to be found without reading through the whole text.

Study Unit created text

These are texts written specifically for the National Curriculum. They are composed of double-page spreads on different aspects of the study unit. Each double page is independent from the previous ones. All the major educational publishers with a history programme for primary pupils have produced non-fiction texts using this format. The way in which the text works marks a considerable change from topic based information books which children may also be using from the library. The structure of topic based information books is likely to be familiar to older primary pupils from their early years reading programme. The topics chosen are generally familiar and the writing is often in a narrative style. The Study Unit created text on the other hand is based on a history topic such as the Tudors, which may be completely unfamiliar to the children. The internal narrative is absent and the children are entirely dependent on the text they read. Ways in which children can be helped to read these texts are discussed later.

Teacher/publisher created fact sheets

Fact sheets are photocopiable sheets providing information about a particular aspect of the history topic. Like many of the Study Unit created texts they may contain follow-up activities for the children to undertake based on the information on the sheet. These are often concerned with comprehension and provide an opportunity for teachers to record children's understanding of written texts. Teachers often create fact sheets on the same aspect of the topic at different reading levels to provide for differentiated needs. One of the major problems with any photocopiable sheet or teacher created work card is that it is likely to be less attractive and less motivating than a colour page spread from a good non-fiction text. Sadly some children's experience of history in the primary school may be largely based on images from photocopies.

CD-ROM

CD-ROM are one of the most exciting resources for history teaching and there are several programmes on the market which can provide children with non-fiction texts supported by original archive material, film, photographs and sound and voice-overs which read the text. One of the major problems in recommending such resources is their rapid development. Publishers' exhibitions, advertisements and reviews in educational publications such as *Child and Junior Education* (Scholastic) and *The Times Educational Supplement,* are the best way of finding out what is on the market. It is also worth looking in children's toy shops because this is where a popular demand for CD-ROM has created a degree of competition. This makes it possible to buy historical CD-ROMs at substantially reduced prices. Les Smart has collected his own and others' promising research into a most constructive book, *Using IT in Primary School History.*

CD-ROM can be divided up into the same categories as other non-fiction. Reference texts include children's encyclopaedias produced by Hutchinson and Dorling Kindersley. Topic based discs cover different Study Units such as Ancient Civilisations – covering Ancient Egypt, Greece and Rome, The Anglo-Saxons and Britain Since 1930. Many of these have been produced for the general consumer, rather than the educational market so have higher readability levels than might be expected.

Surprisingly little work has been done on how children read such texts from the screen although voice-overs do provide a means of access to the text for children who could not cope with it by themselves. When a print-out is made it can provide children with an opportunity to make up their own files, but care needs to be taken that they do actually read the text, rather than just stick it into a file. Print-outs can often be unattractive and demotivating for children who have difficulty reading, particularly those from discs aimed at secondary schools and at the adult market.

Children need to be encouraged to work with a CD-ROM rather than just jump from image to image. Some of the history material examining the remote past is fairly detailed and written for the specialist, rather than the general reader or beginning reader. The most effective CD-ROMs are those using archive material and a clear presentation guide.

Surveying information books

Many children need help in using non-fiction texts. As Neate (1992) made very clear, most children have learnt to read by using narrative texts. Newer reading schemes such as the 'Longman Book Project', Ginn's 'All Aboard' and Collins 'Pathways' contain a number of non-fiction texts among their early readers. But many of these are effectively narrative texts as they require children to read them from cover to cover. The contents may be factual, but the reading strategies are essentially the same as for a narrative text.

The 'Longman Book Project' has two non-fiction boxes, one for each Key Stage. This is edited by Bobbie Neate and a deliberate attempt has been made to provide a series of non-fiction books which teach research skills systematically. The Key Stage 2 box includes a set of books on the Victorians which could be used as a language activity but linked to work being covered in history. Other publishers such as Oxford University Press with their 'Fact Finders' and Heinemann with 'Discovery World' have made a conscious effort to include historical non-fiction texts in their selection of information books.

Using non-fiction texts in history teaching requires children to have some understandings about the differences between narrative and expository texts as well as skills in using different forms of non-fiction texts.

Bobbie Neate provides a good comparison of narrative and expository texts in *Finding Out About Finding Out* (1992).

Structural guiders

One of the main differences with non-fiction texts is that they are not intended to be read through page by page. Children researching into 'court life in Tudor times', for example, need to use the structural guiders provided by the texts to find the exact spot they need. Non-fiction texts contain a variety of structural guiders such as page numbers, glossaries or contents pages. When introducing a new set of history non-fiction texts children could be asked to record the type of structural guiders which they contain.

If children are doing this for the first time try and work with a group and give each child a non-fiction book with the instructions to find out what it is about. Make a note of those children who use structural guiders, such as the details on the back of the book, the contents page and so on as a clue to context, and those who started to read the book from the start to the finish. This gives some sort of base-line in assessing children's levels of research skills and the type of support they will need when working by themselves. Discuss with the children the types of structural guiders they can identify as being useful in finding out what is in the book (and note any which the children do not mention). The children could spend time filling in a matrix and discuss which one has the most useful structural guiders.

EVALUATIVE CRITERIA

The presence or absence of structural guiders is not necessarily the best way to evaluate a non-fiction text. In fact some of the newer texts for early years readers seem overloaded by guiders, which confuse rather than encourage beginning readers.

The best informational texts are written by authors who thoroughly research their subjects, write with imagination and understand the needs and abilities of children (Sutherland and Arbuthnot, 1986). They can be evaluated by six major criteria:

- accuracy and authenticity;
- content and perspective;
- style;
- organisation;
- illustrations and general format;
- support with learning subject specialist vocabulary.

Confident readers are generally able to articulate why they like particular texts and why others do not appeal. When using non-fiction texts they can be encouraged to draw up their own criteria to evaluate texts, both for their appeal and for their usefulness. Such criteria might include questions like:

- Does the book/CD-ROM cover the subject?
- How good are the pictures?
- Can I read the text easily?
- How much information is included?

Bias

In the past history texts have been heavily criticised for the particular viewpoint they represent (Hughes, 1989). History has been seen as the history of the victors, who have tended to be white, male and wealthy. Newer texts are much more aware of the need for an 'inclusive' curriculum for primary history (Claire, 1996), but children need to be taught to identify bias in texts which exclude or marginalise women, children, non-European communities and cultures and the less wealthy. Hilary Claire's book *Reclaiming Our Pasts* provides excellent support for teachers wishing to ensure that equality and diversity are both represented in the primary curriculum.

Exploring how texts work

Exploring how historical texts work provides a functional approach to learning about language. As we use language we develop an implicit understanding of how it works. A functional approach attempts to make this explicit. It helps children to look at how written texts work to enable us to share information, to enquire, to express different points of view, to entertain, to argue, to construct ideas and particularly in history to order our experience and make sense of the world in which we live.

Asking questions

The different texts outlined earlier in the chapter are organised and work in different ways. They all require children to have good library skills so that they can be found initially. Children need to be able to use the structural guiders to find information within the texts, but both of these skills are underdeveloped if children do not learn to ask questions which require the use of the texts.

Since the National Curriculum lays down what children need to know it is relatively easy to think that the questions raised must come from the terms of the document itself. Indeed several school medium-term planning sheets for history are organised in terms of questions. It is however relatively easy, once children become accustomed to asking questions, to get them to raise very similar questions themselves. This gives them an ownership, however artificial, over the curriculum content, which helps to motivate enquiry.

Children sometimes need help asking questions which require research skills to answer them. Questions modelled in the classroom are often those provided by the teacher, for which he or she already knows the answer – 'when did Victoria come to the throne?' – or those from children which involve administration – 'how much should I write?' Genuine knowledge-seeking questions are much rarer and the technique for asking them is often a starting point to encouraging research skills.

The following is an example of one way in which questions can be raised about a unit on Vikings. The example is taken from work carried out in a Year 3 class, where a display of books about the Vikings was laid out for a couple of days without comment.

TEACHER:	What do we know about the Vikings?
PUPILS' RESPONSES:	They did not live like us.
	They did not dress like us.
	They came from Denmark.
	They wore helmets.
	They sailed in longboats.
TEACHER:	What else would we like to know about them?
PUPILS' RESPONSES:	How did they live?
	What did they wear?
	Did they have pets?
	Why did they come?
	When did they come?

Children can then be encouraged to use the non-fiction texts to answer these questions. This can be done individually, in pairs or in groups. Their research may lead them on to asking additional questions.

READING THE TEXTS

Children need to ask appropriate questions, use library skills to find the relevant texts to answer the questions and then use structural guiders to answer the specific question they are focusing on.

The illustration on page 108 indicates some of the challenges presented to children when using an apparently simple text. The page is taken from Hodder's 'History Insights' series on the Tudors. This series is in fact a very good one as it has clear and useful structural guiders, an attractive format and avoids an overuse of different fonts. The problems associated with

Fascinating Facts

The grammar schoolboy's satchel would contain his ink-horn and his quill pen, a knife to make the pen, and some paper, which was too expensive to be supplied by the school. Sand from a sandbox was sprinkled over the page to dry the ink.

technical term not explained in the text

what is Latin?

❝The lady Elizabeth has accomplished her sixteenth year . . . French and Italian she speaks like English; Latin with fluency, propriety and judgement; she also spoke Greek with me, frequently, willingly and moderately. Nothing can be more elegant than her handwriting . . . In music she is very skilful . . .❞

unfamiliar words for most children

From 'The Schoolmaster' (1570), by Roger Ascham, tutor to Princess Elizabeth

Girls attended both the parish school and early years of the grammar schools, but women were not allowed to go to university. Most girls were expected to help in the home and become good housewives. The daughters of wealthier families often learned to read and write from parents, older brothers or governesses. They had visiting tutors for music, dancing and French. Children of the nobility and of royalty were educated at home

technical terms

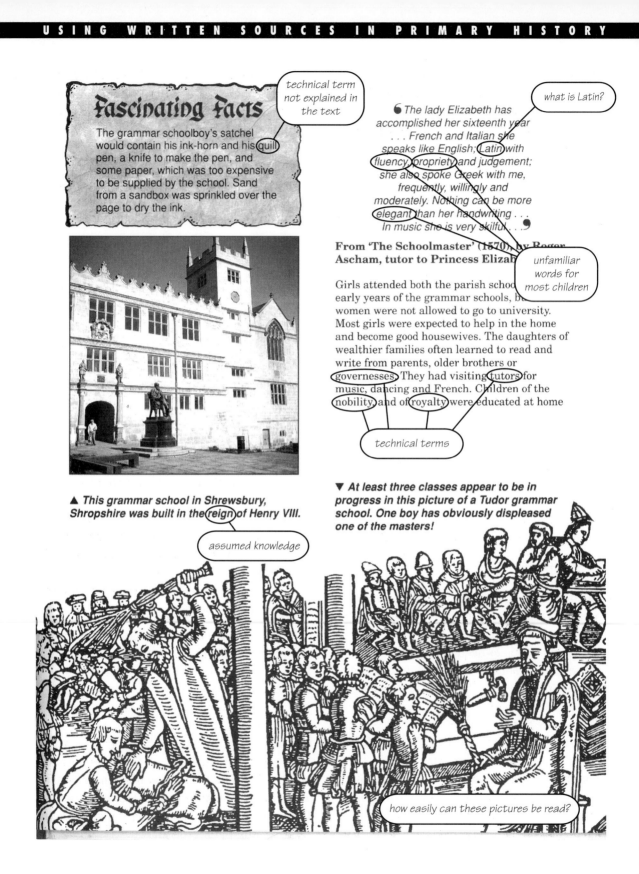

▲ This grammar school in Shrewsbury, Shropshire was built in the reign of Henry VIII.

assumed knowledge

▼ At least three classes appear to be in progress in this picture of a Tudor grammar school. One boy has obviously displeased one of the masters!

how easily can these pictures be read?

both the text and the presentation are a product of history texts and not specific to this one. They indicate several different points which make understanding of such texts more demanding than texts in other areas of the curriculum.

- Pressure on the author to provide a short comprehensive text covering a vast subject on a double-page spread. This means there is no opportunity within the text to explain what technical and unfamiliar words mean (e.g. grammar, priest).
- History texts assume prior knowledge but readers may not have been given any introduction to the subject or any contextual teaching (Neate, 1992). So children may not have come across words such as Shakespeare, quill, governesses, tutors, nobility and royalty.
- The use of written sources from the period using words with which the children may be unfamiliar – in this case fluency, propriety, elegant and Latin.
- Original visual source material may be difficult for children to interpret without help from the text. A double page spread does not allow for this help to be given.
- Current photographs of historic sites such as the sixteenth century grammar school may need some explanation to draw attention to its particularly Tudor characteristics.
- Children are taught to read from left to right across the page. Like most information texts this reads in columns.

TYPES OF READING

One of the reasons some children, and adults, are more able readers than others is because they learn that there are different types of reading. This identification can be encouraged and developed by teachers. The Library Association (1995) suggest that there are six reading strategies:

- Detailed reading – which involves reading a whole passage carefully so that there is complete understanding. Children's early experience of reading develops this skill.
- Skimming – this involves finding out what the passage is about and involves only having a general impression of what the text says.
- Scanning – this means running your eye down the page and looking for specific details.
- Critical readership – this involves separating fact from fiction and often involves some form of decision making. Advanced history texts often involve the reader in this critical interpretation, but many primary texts depend on the text to alert pupils. Looking at a number of written primary sources on a particular topic is often one of the ways in which critical readership is encouraged.
- Analytical reading – this involves studying the writer's techniques and skills so that style and structure can be recognised.
- Reading for enjoyment – reading at your own pace for enjoyment.

Not only do children need practice in developing these different reading strategies, but they need help in identifying them, particularly skimming and scanning when they first use non-fiction texts (Hughes, 1996). Many English text books teach these skills directly, but unless children see and use them in other areas of the curriculum they are unlikely to adopt them as part of their own reading repertoire. Teachers can use texts to model these reading skills and this is one way in which class texts for history can be most profitably used.

Scan it

Write down the dates and names of bicycles mentioned in this passage as quickly as you can.

'The first pedal cycle was the so-called 'boneshaker' which first appeared in 1869. It was found that greater speeds could be achieved with a larger front wheel, so the 'penny-farthing' was introduced in 1879. The real popularity of cycling came with the invention of the 'safety bicycle' in the 1880s. The frame was like a modern bicycle and the pedals drove the back wheel via a chain and 'freewheeling' was now possible. At first the tyres were solid rubber, until in 1888 JB Dunlop invented the tyre with a blow-up inner tube.'

Reading the screen

Using a CD-ROM involves giving children time to explore the software as well as reading the material. Reading about Neil Armstrong's first step on the Moon, becomes much more exciting when it is accompanied by the actual film footage. Schools which have large screens for teaching purposes are at a distinct advantage here as the teacher can then show children some of the facilities available through the CD-ROM. Children can be encouraged to look at particular aspects such as listening to the actual words spoken by Armstrong and the response back at NASA. They can then return to the same piece of film by themselves to look more closely at other aspects.

Reading non-fiction aloud

As well as teaching information retrieval skills it is important for teachers to read non-fiction aloud. In doing this they can

- support the history curriculum
- expand interest in the content areas
- take advantage of a child's spontaneous questions
- stimulate the need to document facts
- create interest in areas totally new to the child
- support writing

- provide practice in finding and researching facts for a project
  (adapted from Burke, E. and Glazer, S. *Using Nonfiction in the Classroom*)

Reading aloud also allows teachers to model a response to non-fiction and make comparisons with fictional texts which may also be read aloud. Extracts from Michael Foreman's *War Boy*, for example, can be compared to a double-page spread on a Study Unit created text on domestic life during the war. Sharing non-fiction with the whole class enables different writing genres to be identified and comparisons made between children's own writings and the genre identified in the text (e.g. diaries).

Historical non-fiction often provides excellent dramatic potential. The teacher can provide the initial stimulus, such as a vivid description about the battle of Thermopylae, and children can then be asked to research for further information about the Spartans so that they could understand why the Persian spy saw them and commented upon combing their hair before battle. The Scholastic Study Kit on the Ancient Greeks provides a much more detailed account of the way in which drama can be used to encourage children to research for more information about the past (page 129, onwards).

Discussing non-fiction

When children are enthusiastic about the topic they need to have an opportunity to be able to share and discuss the ideas they encounter. One of the characteristics of very young able readers of non-fiction is their desire to recite almost word for word what they have just read. Often with no acknowledgement to the original text. Parents, rather than teachers, are often at the receiving end of this which perhaps indicates that recalling written texts orally in school is particularly important for those children who do not have access to many books at home. Talking about a subject helps to clarify key issues and when children are asked to note take they find it easier if they have already become adept at speaking and listening to historical information. A good listener and speaker can often be a good note taker as they learn to field out those pieces of extraneous information which are fed into them.

Teachers often provide the second stage in this exercise by asking for short responses to questions. Skilful questioning (Wragg, 1994) can allow able pupils to show their ability to explore historical ideas, use historical language and interpret historical knowledge.

Burke and Glazer (1994) suggest seven skills which emerge from non-fiction book talk activities:

- expanding ideas beyond those in the text
- working collaboratively
- using resources beyond the text
- using visuals, graphics, illustrations etc
- assessing the quality of non-fiction material
- determining the appropriateness of sources and
- appreciating non-fiction.

Developing skills in communicating knowledge and understanding of history

A considerable amount of work has been done looking at the connection between reading and writing expository texts; but until recently most of this was carried out in secondary schools. Sydney Wood in an article in *Language and Learning* (1995) points out that the types of assessment used in history involve children absorbing considerable quantities of heavily text-based material in order to undertake writing tasks. He suggests that two key issues emerge from this. Firstly that pupils are engaged in 'reading to write' and coming directly from this they need to 'reflect on the writer's ideas and craft'.

Developing skills in communicating historical knowledge and understanding involves children in being able to read and write informational, narrative and imaginative texts using a wide variety of different genres. Wood suggests that this process involves:

- Knowledge and understanding of the topic that pupils bring to the writing task, both general knowledge and history-specific knowledge;
- The difficulty of the task – i.e. whether it is a narrative, descriptive, expository and whether the genre required is different from the genre of the text;
- The task explained – how clearly the task is explained, how purposeful the activity is and for whom the writing is intended;
- Text to be used – the process is different when a number of texts are used, rather than just one; how long the texts are and the level of language difficulty.

Note making

Neate (1992) suggests that there are several strategies which can be adopted to make note making effective for primary pupils and there is no one superior method. She suggests summarising, outlining, underlining, crossing out, tabulation, modelling and patterning. Her own research work found that underlining was the most effective strategy to use with young children as a starting point to effective note making. She also recommends modelling, which at a very simple level involves careful drawing from a written text. There are obvious problems with its use in history as children have limited historical language and illustrations alongside the text are often key elements in helping children to understand difficult concepts.

Using world written sources

All the sources considered in previous chapters have been about British history, and in particular about those aspects of British history which figure in the current version of the English National Curriculum. There are three reasons for this. Firstly, they are mostly in a language comprehensible to young children and their teachers, or translated from Latin or Anglo-Saxon or a Norse tongue but with reference to a country familiar to nearly all the children. Secondly, with increasing force as we approach recent times, there are very many of them: the problem is often that there are so many that it is difficult to make a sensible choice among this profusion. Thirdly, and most importantly, they are about the nearest part of the world, the part that children know best. That is why British history has figured so prominently in this book; not because it is 'better', but because it is nearer.

However, one important purpose of primary History, recognised in the National Curriculum itself, is to combat insularity and parochialism, to open up horizons and, in concert with the 'distant places' of the Geography curriculum, to stimulate the challenge of the remote in place and time. The study of Ancient Greece is compulsory, and there is also a choice of one 'non-European civilisation' whether of great antiquity or of comparative modernity: Ancient Egypt, Mesopotamia, the Indus Valley, the Maya, the kingdom of Benin or the Aztecs. If written sources can enrich the understanding of British history, surely they should have the same value for this wider purpose?

They do; but to a much more limited extent.

Except for Commonwealth countries and the USA, written sources including inscriptions are usually in other languages, and sometimes in other scripts, though these can, of course be transcribed and translated. Even so, most of these are not readily accessible. In any case they can rarely be supplemented by material found by teachers, as is often possible with the British material, where parish records, inventories, street directories and news reports can be sought out. But many of these non-British sources, such as Egyptian hieroglyphics, Mesopotamian cuneiform writing, and the Hebrew or Greek alphabet are interesting in themselves, and many schools do develop work on them.

Teachers often link such work with a more general language topic on Communications, including some consideration of the history of writing and printing. Some also take other scripts familiar to some of the children – Arabic, Cyrillic, Urdu – and encourage all the children to use them, sometimes in relation to religious education. Extracts from some actual written sources such as the *Egyptian Book of the Dead*, and inscriptions on rocks, pillars and tablets, have survived and are made available in information books for children, and teachers have developed stimulating work using material of this kind. Often, such 'written' material as is suitable has been introduced, effectively, into the books and packs prepared by publishers for Key Stage 2, in relation to other evidence about non-European civilisations. There, it is found alongside material about architecture, artefacts, pottery, grave furniture, surviving beliefs and customs as in

Benin and with the Maya, and what is known about early discoveries in mathematics, science and technology. Such repertoires of information provide something which children can recognise as relevant to their own experience.

One of the non-British elements in the Key Stage 2 curriculum which schools must offer is **Ancient Greece**. In respect of written sources, this is rather different from the non-European civilisations. For extensive Greek writings have survived, in the shape of myth, drama, literature, poetry, philosophy and history itself. All of these are part of the heritage of Ancient Greece, and constitute one important reason why Ancient Greece is widely considered important in a history curriculum. Certainly modern Europe, including modern Britain, owes a substantial part of its cultural heritage to Ancient Greece. In England, the long legacy of classical education has perhaps led to the dubious assumption that Greek culture could be understood by young minds, before they were capable of appreciating its more abstract qualities or its significance.

Yet in fact the history of Ancient Greece is not easy to illuminate by direct quotation from written sources, however vivid the translation. A snatch of the *Iliad* may perhaps convey something of the atmosphere of that semi-mythical world in which mortals and immortals were mixed together, but for the most part the narrative of Ancient Greece, where relevant, is probably better taken from modern versions specially prepared for younger readers than from any translation, however vivid, of the original texts.

So probably the approach to Ancient Greece should be undertaken on much the same lines as for the 'non-European' examples. It should incorporate only the minimum of written sources among the other significant but more comprehensible and appealing elements in Greek culture. These are: myths and legends in simplified form, architecture, pottery and other artefacts, costume, contributions to mathematics and science, and the nearest acceptable approach to written records, the Greek alphabet itself, and

words of Greek origin in common or technical parlance. Here there are many examples of excellent work in which children can understand the content of what they learn. They can also relate much of it to other parts of the curriculum including English and art and drama (wearing a chiton or armed as a hoplite) and to the world outside: Greek influences on Victorian architecture, Greek personal names, holidays in modern Greece, and so on. This is a rich introduction for Key Stage 2, but one to which original written sources can contribute only marginally. There may be exceptional teachers with exceptional classes who might be able to make Pericles' *Funeral Oration* live for them and awaken the beginnings of critical thinking about politics and society; but for most young children such issues lie in the future.

There are other 'past societies' not mentioned in the present National Curriculum for young children, which might give more scope for using written sources. Although drastic selection would be necessary, sufficient examples in the English language could be found from the journals and diaries of statesmen and generals and explorers across the centuries, as we did for Drake in Chapter 5. These could be supplemented, for more recent and more literate years, by material about ordinary folk across the English-speaking world, and by extracts from literature in English, for example from the Caribbean, from West Africa, or from the Indian sub-continent, used to illuminate studies of particular people in particular places in which history, geography, languages, art, music and dance could all be represented. More recent non-English-speaking cultures, European and other, could also figure, with a few words of another language learned. These immense possibilities are mentioned simply to emphasise our awareness of their significance for the education of younger children.

In any case they must lie beyond the scope of this book. Meanwhile we hope that the examples and suggestions which we have given will stimulate teachers to envisage the possibilities that do lie open to them; to find other sources; and to devise other ways of using them. There is much to be achieved with material near at hand, within and outside the parts of British history considered in this book, provided that we convey to children that it is just one small part of the immense history of humanity.

Record Office work

Four Education Officers at Record Offices – Ian Mason (Essex), David Bond (Hampshire), James Turtle (Gloucestershire) and Mary Mason (Wolverhampton) – have written accounts of their work with primary age children specially for this book. This work has been carried out both in classrooms and in Record Offices themselves. With the Essex example, the relevant documents have also been reproduced. Record Officers in many parts of the country offer help to primary teachers based on similar local and regional records.

1   WORKING WITH INFANTS (ESSEX RECORD OFFICE SCHOOLS SERVICE)

One of the successes of the national curriculum in history has been the recognition given to the fact that classes of very young children may get something out of history. By extension this means that young children may benefit too from the raw material of history, i.e. archival material. Thanks to the 'key elements' of Key Stage 1, which speak of *written accounts, pictures and photographs and written sources*, increasing numbers of teachers have been emboldened to ask for assistance from their Essex Record Office. What written sources can possibly be accessed by five and six year-olds? If the children are unable to read, surely then there is little point in difficult originals? To counter a natural scepticism and without a context for such work, and to perform that important task of capturing interest, I would put before teacher and taught a page of the *Accounts of a Schoolboy, 1759*, [E.R.O. reference D/DBy F17]. This is working on the principles that children are curious about other children and that new information makes more sense and fits in, if it relates to their present concerns. The assumption that originals are too difficult for young children is a prejudice that needs challenging. Left alone and unaided, of course

most young children will struggle. But working as a group and with an enthusiast to act as a guide, things may be delightfully otherwise. There is surprisingly little difficulty when interesting pieces of the text are highlighted or pointed out and provided that many accompanying explanations are forthcoming from the teacher or Archive Education Officer. 'Without looking, what do you think Richard Aldsworth would spend much of his pocket money on, so long ago?' Substitute 'sugar candy' for 'sweets' and yes, there you have the entry supporting your guess. Can you see it by the numbers '0-0-6' in the document?.

What jobs do we want archival sources to perform for us in a very short time? Teachers, wary of the unknown, are often anxious that groups of infants be addressed for only a very limited spell, say ten or fifteen minutes. But with the aid of video-tape to show where and how the originals are safely kept and with the presence of a two hundred year old parish chest nearby and objects related to writings, like quills, slates, or ink-holders to hand, it is not unusual for young children to want a session to extend for up to an hour. Do not we all enjoy a change of voice and pace, whatever the pretext?

What may be *begun* with young children, once passed the mythical barrier of disinterest and the exaggerated hurdle of difficulty? There is something to add to the children's growing awareness of the concept of 'old'. A *small chronological sequence of sources* may be set out in their room and children may pass along in front of it. A fragment of a medieval Bible on parchment can be seen alongside sixteenth century account books, a seventeenth century paper inventory, eighteenth century notebook, nineteenth century ledger and twentieth century pocket diary (underneath their protective 'melanex' screens of course). Changing materials are enjoyed. A delight is taken in the care with which illuminated letters were made. The fantastic shapes in coloured ink of marbled 'paste-downs' are fascinating, as is the tiny thrill of looking where we usually should not be looking. It is fun to go beyond forbidding brass clasps and locks and to look into private diaries or 'official' papers, like a headteacher's log-book. A little of the awe or the shock of the past can be introduced? A sequence of postmen in their evolving uniforms set beside a large blow-up of the penny black postage stamp, and a photograph of an old post-van delivering air-mail to a bi-plane serve very well in Essex (E.R.O. reference T/Z 54/7-13).

What central historical concepts may be un-packed from photographs or illustrations? A too-heavy concentration on writings will weary any of us, whatever our age. *The Broken Flowerpot* has proved a useful image in un-picking what children make of events and causation, especially when our evidence is *post facto*. This is a posed photograph by Fred Spalding of a child holding a damaged plant-pot, while an adult is standing by holding the damaged plant and root-ball. At first glance, many children 'blame' the child for the broken pot, the 'event'. At a second look, they

begin to appreciate that the adult may have been involved. When prompted by questioning, children may suggest an agent who would not wait around to be photographed, like a cat, or an agency that is difficult to photograph, such as the wind. The continuities of history can be gleaned from images of school-children playing leap-frog in the late Victorian playground, of *Woodham Ferrers National School.*

A hint of the different interpretations of history and a small appreciation of the impact of differing view-points may follow from a shared reading of a few words of a reminiscence about a flood. Why would the author of 'Things I Remember of Chelmsford', 1888 [T/Z 25/3], speak as a child of 'a glorious sight'? 'Faggots of wood, buckets, baths all floating about in the back of the house and, in the road, were men in boats!' Would a mother and father have thought differently of the flood than this child?

Why cannot the complexities of historical evidence be enjoyed from the start? Not everything written or in print may be taken at face value. *The 1992 Note from a Tiptree Mum* in a lunch box: 'Fiona, eat your crust or you will be in big trouble' may be 'read between the lines' and seen as an expression of love and humour, rather than as the literal words of a threat. Not everything written or in print is to be believed entirely. The *1754 Dictionary of Arts and Sciences* with its mistaken image of a hippopotamus can be critically appreciated by the young. How do they know this engraving is false? Why might the artist have shown this animal with claws and canine teeth and thus have 'got it wrong'? Which books and what sorts of information may be 'wrong' or provisional in our own school libraries?

Stories from and about the past are to be enjoyed, even if someone else has to introduce, read and explain most of them. Recognising even if reluctantly, that the whole of human experience

Accounts of a Schoolboy, 1759 (a 'gig' is a whipping top)

is not to be explained through E.R.O. sources I have enjoyed bringing the attention of the class back together after a lively session exploring documents with a tale such as Rogers, P. and Johnson, J., *From Me to You*, (Orchard Books, £6.95, ISBN 1 85213 0350). As with many classroom tactics this was picked up from good colleagues who allowed me to remain with them and their classes as they continued with their lessons. There are so many good stories. Some may be picked up for 10 pence at jumble sales, as Marten and Carter's was. Others are more expensive like West, J. and West, M., *Magic Map – The Infant Telltale*, (1991, Elm Publications, ISBN 1 85450 008 2, £8.95).

Archives may happily produce support materials for the popular themes of Key Stage 1: 'people who help us'; 'communications', 'shops and shopping' or 'houses and homes'. And if young children enjoy sharing an interest in collectors and collecting, while they are beginning their history, and if this leads to a readiness to accept the duty of preserving some things and supporting archives along the way, then so much the better [see Newberry, E., *Collect it! Making Collections from Fossils to Fakes*, [1991, A. & C. Black, ISBN 0 7136 3470 7, £7.99].

IAN C. MASON, ARCHIVE EDUCATION OFFICER,
ESSEX RECORD OFFICE

2 WORK DONE WITH TEACHERS AT HAMPSHIRE RECORD OFFICE

Hampshire County Council has provided an archive education service for schools and colleges since the early 1980s, based at Hampshire Record Office, Winchester. The work of David Bond, the Archive Education Officer, falls into two distinct areas: providing direct support for teachers and student teachers who visit Hampshire Record Office, and producing resource material for use within primary schools and teacher training colleges throughout Hampshire and neighbouring counties.

In-Service training is provided for teachers and student teachers at Hampshire Record Office, as well as within Hampshire County Council's

A trew Inventory of John Garards Goods taken Jan. ye 20 : 1715

6

Imprimis one flock bed and bedstead one bolsted 2 fether pillowes 2 blanketts one Rug 4 Chaires one worming pan one kettle one lantorn : one tunne one Chest one hutch one Cobard one brode mug one Jugg one saspan 4 peuter spones one Trammell 2 wooden platters one bill one Ax one paile one form one table one stoole 2 hammars one skillitt 2 bottles one iron Candlestick one Sack one light Coat and wastcoat 2 pair briches one sad Collerd greatcoat 2 pair of sheets one (blank) one baskett one wigg one fier-sheuvell.

(Endorsed:) Jery Garards.

Inventory of a pauper's goods 1715 (a 'trammell' was a hook in the fireplace to hold a kettle, and a 'skillitt was a small metal pot with a long handle [Essex Record Office, reference D/P 30/18/4 Witham]

Divisional Professional Centres, and through twilight cluster meetings in the county's schools. Help and advice is given in a number of areas, such as how to access appropriate material from the record office's huge and varied collections, and how to undertake a local study using original documents alongside the physical evidence of artefacts, buildings and sites. An emphasis is placed upon combining the written and visual sources to be found at the Record Office, with archaeological and ephemeral sources to be found in Hampshire's museums and at historic sites across the county.

Groups of teachers and students who visit the Record Office are first of all given an introductory talk on the nature of material held at Hampshire Record Office, followed by a short video on how to use the finding aids in the Record Office searchroom, and, most important of all, they are able to handle original documents for themselves and discuss ways in which the information, written and visual, contained within the documents can be effectively used in a classroom situation. Similar sessions, using facsimiles, are also held in teacher centres and schools where it is not practical to transport original documents. Finally, groups are informed of the variety of services offered to schools and colleges through the Archive Education Service at Hampshire Record Office. These include being able to provide resource packs of photocopied material for use in schools on a wide range of subjects appropriate to the National Curriculum.

A series of approaches to the use of archive material in schools has been developed at Hampshire Record Office, so that teachers can choose what is most appropriate to their needs. Resource packs and videos have been produced which can be used by all schools in their own classrooms, and local study material covering a limited range of sources can be tailored to the needs of individual schools. For those teachers with a commitment and interest to develop their own material, more detailed guidance can be given, and sets of photocopied documents on a variety of themes and locations within Hampshire have been compiled to help teachers produce their own resources.

It is acknowledged that not all teachers have a specialist background in history, so a number of resource packs and videos have been produced with the requirements of the National Curriculum in mind. These resources obviate the need for a specialist knowledge of the Medieval, Tudor or Victorian periods, or Twentieth Century British history. A pre-selected collection of photographs and documents is contained within each resource pack, complete with detailed teachers notes on the material itself and suggestions on how they might use it in the classroom. As well as providing resources for Key Stage 2 on the core study unit Life in Tudor Times, there are document packs and videos available on broader subjects including 300 Years of Land Transport, and 100 Years of Shops & Shopping. The needs of Key Stage 1 pupils have not been overlooked, and the resource pack relating to the life of Florence Nightingale has proved very popular with primary schools.

The needs of primary school pupils can generally be met from the resources mentioned above, and school group visits to the record office are normally arranged for older pupils at Key Stages 4 and above. We encourage these pupils to become fully-fledged public users of archival material, able to work on their own initiative in the Record Office searchroom.

INSET DAY WITH PRIMARY TEACHERS AT HAMPSHIRE RECORD OFFICE

Primary school teachers, and student teachers, often need to be convinced that Record Offices have something to offer younger children. They tend to assume that many of the documents held in Record Offices are inaccessible, partly because they are written sources, and partly because they are too 'adult' and therefore inappropriate. An activity which is used at Hampshire Record Office, which originated at an INSET day for primary teachers has proved to be a popular introduction for teachers and students needing to work with archival sources. The activity begins with a reading of *Our House*, by Emma and Paul Rogers (Walker Books), which tells the story of a house and its occupants since it was built in the 1780s, almost to the present day. The last of four family stories in the book shows how items from the past can tell us something about a house's former occupants. With this in mind our activity then looks at how documentary evidence can also tell us about people living in the past.

The activity continues by examining a photograph of two young children 'discovered' in an envelope. The envelope is addressed, in this case, to Mr Walter Bailey, Caer Gwent, Abbey Hill Road, Winchester. There is a Victorian penny black stamp on the envelope. The photograph inside shows two children in Victorian clothes, and on the reverse are written in ink the names Hilda and Maude, and the date 1885. The group is asked to discuss the envelope and photograph and speculate on who Walter Bailey, and Hilda and Maude might be based upon the limited evidence available. The discussion usually includes trying to work out how old the children were at the time of the photograph.

New evidence is then presented to the group in stages. First of all, an extract from a trade directory of 1901 is used, which shows that Walter Bailey was at this time a solicitor and Town Clerk of Winchester. Discussions about how important a person Mr Bailey might have been then takes

place, including what type of house he might have lived in. Secondly, a copy of an estate agent's brochure, complete with photography, for the sale of Caer Gwent is considered. Does the house fit the group's interpretation? Next, a 25" scale Ordnance Survey map is used to locate the property. It is now clear that Mr Bailey's house was a large detached villa on the outskirts of Winchester.

The group will want to know more about the children in the photograph. Were they Mr Bailey's children, and were the group correct in their guesses about their ages? Using the 1891 census the group discovered Caer Gwent and amongst its occupants were Mr Walter Bailey and three children including two named Hilda and Maude. Further examination shows that the family had a number of domestic servants, including a governess and children's maid. This leads to a discussion on life 'upstairs and downstairs', and suggestions for further activities such as role play using Victorian costumes and handling museum artefacts. More information on the family was found using parish registers, including the marriage of Mr and Mrs Bailey, and the baptisms of their children. Having established a limited 'family tree' for the Bailey family, the group compares Victorian families with modern-day families, by looking at such things as the number of children (size of nuclear family), lifestyle (domestic employment and pre-school education) and occupations.

Having learnt something on the topic of *Our House*, the group can then pursue their enquiries into Victorian family life by looking at schools and churches in Victorian times, using a variety of sources at the Record Office including school log books, parish registers and photographs. This is a fairly easy exercise for teachers to put together for themselves, based perhaps on an old house near the school. The exercise draws on a number of standard sources to be found in most record offices – maps, trade directories, census returns, parish registers, photographs, school records etc. The type of house can be varied, from a well-to-do family living in a large detached house with servants, to a more humble working-class family living in a terraced house or cottage. The activity could even encompass other building types such as Our School or Our Church.

DAVID BOND
ARCHIVE EDUCATION OFFICER

3   GLOUCESTERSHIRE RECORD OFFICE: ARCHIVES EDUCATION SERVICE

The Record Office appointed its first full-time Archives Education Officer in April 1991, replacing a part-time seconded post. The work of the Archives Education Officer with primary schools can be divided into four main areas:

1   *Providing resource packs*

This involves identifying and copying suitable items for classroom use, mostly to support the Key Stage 2 local study as well as the units on the Victorians, Britain Since 1930 and the Tudors. Schools requesting resources have a package selected for their individual area. For a primary school such a package will typically contain about 15 pages of 1851 Census, 25"–1 mile Victorian O.S. maps (full A/O size sheets), extracts from Kelly's Directory, school log book entries and World War II evacuee register, sale particulars, photographs, parish registers, 1608 militia review (printed), two or three 16/17th C. probate inventories (transcribed with glossary), together with whatever else seems of use and interest.

The Archives Education Officer will take a completed package out to a school and spend an hour or so going through it with the teacher(s). In the production of primary school packages, the Archives Education Officer is assisted by the voluntary work of a retired primary school teacher who visits the Office once a week and whose assistance has been invaluable.

In addition to individual packages, there are a number of small 'off-the-peg' packages on popular topics such as 'Gloucester Docks' and 'Regency Cheltenham'. Maps and photographs are also provided for Key Stage 1.

2   *Offering In-Service training*

Introducing teachers to archive material, and to practical ideas for learning activities, is essential to implementing its use in the classroom. The Archives Education Officer offers day-courses for primary teachers, in collaboration with the LEA and the local College of Higher Education, as well as participating on request in schools' own INSET activities.

3   *Organising group visits to the Record Office*

Gloucestershire Record Office is fortunate in being able to accommodate visits without interrupting the normal work of the Office. A typical half-day visit includes a video introduction to the work of the Record Office, a tour of the building and a session working on specially selected documents.

4   *Teaching*

The Archives Education Officer will visit schools on request to work alongside a teacher with a class using archive material. Although the number of such requests is relatively small, it is an important part of supporting the use of archive materials in the classroom and of trying out different ideas for activities.

Until September 1996 the Archives Education Officer's time was free to maintained schools in Gloucestershire, although there was a charge to cover the cost of copying (typically about £30 for a primary school pack). Primary schools now have to decide whether they wish to pay an annual subscription (£20–£50 depending on the size of the school) or pay charges for the service as they use it.

'THERE ISN'T ANY HISTORY ROUND US!': A CASE STUDY

Warden Hill is a typical modern suburban housing-estate on the edge of Cheltenham. The 1888 OS map shows only fields, paths, a railway line (now gone) and the small farm after which the estate and school are named. With the help of this map, and copies of other documents from Gloucestershire Record Office, Year 6 children were able to build up a picture of the time before the estate was built.

John Lees, their teacher, drew an overlay for the map showing the modern lay-out of roads and houses so that the children could easily see how much had changed. Kelly's Directory for 1897 identified the farmer as Philip Weaver, and the 1891 Census gave more details: Philip and Joyce Weaver had eight children and farmed only 26 acres. The children were surprised that such a small farm could support so large a family! The Weavers were also on the 1881 Census, but were not there in 1871. Since the Census showed that their eldest child was born in the parish in 1872, there was a clue that Philip had moved to Warden Hill at about that time.

The next document was an estate agent's sale particular for 1920, when the estate of which Warden Hill was part was auctioned. From this the children learnt that the Weavers were tenants and deduced that Philip must have died because Joyce was then paying the rent of £62 per year. A note enclosed showed that Harry Weaver, one of Philip and Joyce's sons, bought the farm for £825. Because he needed a mortgage, a survey and valuation were made by the same estate agents giving details of the farm and buildings. The children were able to identify exactly which fields belonged to the farm and made another overlay for the OS map. A reference to a right-of-way in the survey confirmed that the Weavers had moved to Warden Hill in 1872.

While the children were doing their investigation, it became clear that a Mr Weaver who lived near the school was Harry's nephew. He came into class to tell the children about his visits to the farm as a boy, during World War II, and how two of his aunts (shown on the 1891 Census) continued to live there until 1960 when the land was sold for re-development.

Finally, the children walked down to the site. Although the farmhouse and buildings have been demolished, traces of them can still clearly be seen as that part of the farm has not yet been built on. Combining physical, oral and documentary evidence not only helped the children to learn about their home area, but the different types of evidence brought each other to life.

JAMES TURTLE
ARCHIVES EDUCATION OFFICER

4   WOLVERHAMPTON ARCHIVES AND LOCAL STUDIES EDUCATION SERVICE

**Wolverhampton Archives and Local Studies,
42–50, Snow Hill, Wolverhampton WV2 4AG
Telephone 01902 717703**

An education officer is employed at Wolverhampton and provides a service to educational users of all ages. The education officer, Mary Mills, is a former teacher and also works as a member of the archives staff.

The education service is provided free of charge to Wolverhampton LEA schools. Schools who have opted out, or are from neighbouring authorities, e.g. Staffordshire, can have the same service but are charged.

The main task of the education officer is to respond to requests from teachers. She offers advice on resourcing topics, recommending appropriate materials from the archives and local studies and providing photocopies where copyright and the condition of the document allows. This is generally done by inviting the teacher or group of teachers into the archives and showing them a selection of sources from which they can choose what best fits in with their project. This approach also allows the education officer to suggest alternative lines of research which may not have occurred to the teacher, particularly when she is consulted at the planning stage. Advice can also be given on how to use the sources in the classroom.

When the topic is a local study of the area around the school, often involving history and geography, she often takes a collection of maps, photographs, trade directories, census material and relevant documents to show to the whole staff during a curriculum development session. They then select materials to copy in order to start off a bank of materials for future use.

The education officer frequently visits schools with original sources to work with pupils, either in small groups or whole classes. Again the more involvement the teacher has the better and they generally either visit the archives beforehand to see the materials and take copies for follow up work, or listen to the talk with the pupils and take copies afterwards. Visits can also be arranged to the archives where groups can learn about the work we do or carry out research from sources. These visits need to be carefully structured so that pupils learn how interesting the material is, but also appreciate the importance of the rules and regulations employed by record offices in order to preserve the archives in their care.

Training days are organised through the LEA Inset programme including some in conjunction with curriculum support staff. Some of these courses are aimed specifically at Early Years teachers and those attending have included nursery school staff. Teachers are generally given information about what material we have, time to select sources relevant to their own schools and ideas on how to use sources in a classroom situation including utilising information technology to make sources more accessible to pupils.

The concept keyboard is a particularly useful tool for younger pupils and a publication called *The Changing Face of Dudley Street* has been produced based on a commercial programme called *Time Tunnel* and concentrating on Wolverhampton's main shopping street. Other publications aimed at primary schools include a document pack on the day Queen Victoria visited Wolverhampton and a history of Wolverhampton through maps with an accompanying teachers' booklet.

Case studies

1   Ettingshall Infants Year 1
The teacher based a study of the history of the school and local area around some old photographs she found at school and a section of cobbles in a corner of the playground.

One photograph shows the original school building, nicknamed the *Tin School* and one a school May Queen, Elsie Gannor, pictured in 1926. The teacher asked me to provide maps, and photographs and used them to 'construct' a family for Elsie. Thus the photograph of a miner's cottage became the home Elsie's family had lived in; a photograph of a mine, the place her grandfather worked etc.

I have some reservations about such manipulating of material but can appreciate how it can help to focus information for very young children. I often suggest that if infants teachers want to use census they just look at one household who lived in a house that is still standing. If there is an old photograph of the house even better and if there are people in the street it is possible to speculate on who they might be.

The pupils also looked at how the school buildings had developed using school photographs and a series of 25" to the mile OS maps. I had 2 small groups of pupils, selected by the teacher, to look at maps with me. Although the teacher felt they could only cope with looking at the school buildings they soon began asking questions about the surrounding area and seemed quite able to follow when I showed them rows of houses, streets, the railway (which runs alongside the playground) and the small coal pits dotted around. The teacher did some follow up work on street names.

2 Graiseley Infants Year 2

The teacher here walked her pupils around the immediate neighbourhood of the school; an area containing some Victorian houses, a public house and some old factories but bounded by a recently constructed ring road and retail development. She then asked me to bring in old photographs, maps, a trade directory and census material. The children were basically asked to find things that had changed and things that were the same and examined one Victorian household.

I looked at 3 photographs with them taken from roughly the same place in the 1900s, 1960s and 1970s. We looked in more detail at the Victorian photograph noting obvious things such as the horse and cart, the clothes, the pram etc. We also speculated on who the little boy was with and what he was doing and tried to find him and his family on a page of census for this road. It was again a rather manipulated exercise as I had carefully chosen a page with a suitable family on it but it led to discussion on ages, rich and poor etc and, I think, gave them some idea of how you can get information from sources.

Both of these schools are in inner-city type areas and Graiseley in particular has a large proportion of children from different ethnic origins.

MARY MILLS
ARCHIVES EDUCATION OFFICER

Bibliography

Limited to titles specially related to the contents of this book.
* suitable for primary school children to read. Further children's books relevant to Chapters 3 to 8 are listed under Chapter 9.

General (not a full list of books on primary history)

ANDREETI, K. (1993) *Teaching History from Primary Evidence* (ch. 7). David Fulton.

BLYTH, J. (1990) *History in Primary Schools (pp. 120–47).* Open University Press.

BLYTH, J. (1994) *History 5 to 11* (pp. 80–9). Hodder & Stoughton Educational.

COOPER, H. (1995) *The Teaching of History* (pp. 113–14). David Fulton.

COULSON, I. and CRAWFORD, A. (eds) (1995) *Archives in Education.* Archive Society Publications No. 1, Public Record Office.

DAVIES, I and WEBB, C. (1996) *Using Documents.* English Heritage.

HAIGH, C. (1985) *The Cambridge Historical Encyclopaedia of Great Britain and Ireland.* Cambridge University Press.

HMSO (1995) *History in the National Curriculum.*

HUGHES, P. and TWEEDIE, P. (1992) *Historical Maps, Starting History.* Scholastic Publications.

MUMBY, L. H. (ed.) (1994) *Short Guide to Records.* Historical Association.

PURKIS, S. (1995) *A Teacher's Guide to Using Memorials.* English Heritage.

SMART, L. (1995) *Using IT in Primary School History.* Cassell.

Timeline: 3500 BC–AD 2000 (1996) Pictorial Charts Educational Trust.

Chapter 1: Written sources and historical thinking skills

HMSO (1991) *History in the National Curriculum.*

SCAA (1995) *Planning the Curriculum at Key Stages 1 and 2.*

SCAA (1996) *Desirable Outcomes for Children's Learning on Entering Compulsory Education.*

Chapter 2: Starting points

*AHLBERG, J. and A. (1983) *Peepo.* Picture Puffins.

*AHLBERG, J. and A. (1988) *Starting School.* Picture Puffins.

*CATLEY, A. (1989) *Jack's Basket.* Beaver.

*DUPASQUIER, P. (1987) *Our House on the Hill.* Picture Puffins.

*DUPASQUIER, P. (1989) *The Garage. The Airport. The Building Site. The Railway Station. The Harbour. The Factory.* Walker Books.

*GALBRAITH, K. (1990) *Laura Charlotte.* Hutchinson.

*GOULD, D. (1990) *Grandpa's Slide Show.* Picture Puffins.

*GRAY, N. and RAY, J. (1988) *A Balloon for Grandad.* Orchard Books.

HARNETT, P. (1993) 'Identifying progression in children's understanding: the use of visual materials to assess primary school children's learning of History', *Cambridge Journal of Education* (23, 2).

LYNN, S. (1993) 'Children's reading pictures: History visuals at Key Stages 1 and 2', *Education 3–13* (21, 3, pp. 23–9).

*McKEE, D. (1987) *Two Monsters* and *Tusk, Tusk.* Beaver.

*OBERMAN, S. and LEWIN, T. (1988) *Always Adam.* Gollancz.

*SHELDON, J. (1990) *The Whale's Song.* Hutchinson.

*WADDELL, M. (1990) *Grandma's Bill.* Simon & Schuster.

*WADDELL, M. and READ, N. (1991) *Coming Home.* Simon & Schuster.

Chapter 3: Key Stage 1

ALTON, G. (1985) *The Great Fire of London.* Tressell.

ESSEX RECORD OFFICE (1996) *An Essex Pack of Historical Sources for Key Stage 1*

BACKHOUSE, J. (1979) *The Illuminated Manuscript.* Phaidon.

DUCHESS OF YORK and STONEY, M. (1991) *Victoria and Albert: Life at Osborne House.* Weidenfeld & Nicolson.

FULFORD, R. (1951) *Queen Victoria* (Brief Lives) Collins.

*MICHELHILL, B. (1991) *Princess Victoria.* Ginn.

*MIDDLETON, G. (1969) *At the Time of the Plague and the Fire.* Longman.

*MURPHY, E. (1962) *Samuel Pepys in London.* Longman.

POST, C. and M. (1974) *Royal Portraits from the Plea Rolls.* HMSO.

*REYNOLDS, R. and SMITH, J. (1991) *Elizabeth I* (Sunshine Series). Heinemann.

*ROGERS, E. and R. (1992) *Our House.* Walker Books.

ROUTH, C. R. N. and BAILEY, R. (1956) *They Saw it Happen: 1485–1688.* Blackwell.

SEAC (1993–94) *Children's Work Assessed: History and Geography.*

STRACHEY, L. (1936) *Queen Victoria.* Chatto & Windus.

NCC (1993) *Teaching History at Key Stage 1.*

*THOMSON, R. (1992) *Changing Times.* Franklin Watts.

Chapter 4: Romans, Anglo-Saxons and Vikings in Britain

The Anglo-Saxon Chronicle (1938 edition). Everyman Library. Dent.

BEDE (Venerable) (1939 edition) *Ecclesiastical History of the English Nation*. Everyman Library. Dent.

EKWALL, E. (1940) *Concise Oxford Dictionary of English Place Names* (2nd edn). Oxford University Press (see also MILLS, A. D., under Chapter 10).

FARMER, A. and EWING, A. (1992) *Teaching the Romans in Britain at Key Stage 2* (Bringing History to Life). Historical Association.

*FINCHAM, R. (1976) *Roman Britain and the Saxon Shore*. Chambers.

*HARDMAN, M. (ed.) (1996) *Roman Chester* pack. Chester Education, Grosvenor Museum, Chester.

*JONES, T. (1983) *The Saga of Eric the Viking*. Puffin (not about KING Eric).

*LIVERSEDGE, J. (1983) *Roman Britain*. Longman.

MAGNUSSON, M. (1980) *Vikings!* BBC Publications.

MATTINGLY, H. (1948) *Tacitus on Britain and Germany*. Penguin Books.

ORDNANCE SURVEY (1994) *Map of Roman Britain* from Ordnance Survey, Romsey Road, Maybush, Southampton SO16 4GU. (If obtainable, their maps of *Ancient Britain* would also be worth consulting. *Britain in the Dark Ages* is no longer available, but old copies may be found in some libraries.)

STURLUSSON, SNORRI (1930 edition) *Sagas of the Norse Kings*. (Everyman Library). Dent.

Chapter 5: Britain in Tudor times

Leland's *Itinerary*, Camden's *Britannia* and William Harrison's *Description of England* may be found in a few public libraries, or perhaps consulted through inter-library loans. It is often more practical to look in local history sections or elsewhere for references to these general 'period' accounts.

IRWIN, M. (1944) *Young Bess* (1950) *Elizabeth, the Captive Princess* (1959) *Elizabeth and the Prince of Spain*. Chatto & Windus.

PRESCOT, H. M. P. (1953) *The Man on a Donkey*. Eyre and Spottiswoode (about the Dissolution of the monasteries).

*REES, D. (1982) *The House that Moved*. Puffin.

ROUTH, C. R. N. and BAILEY, R. (1956) *They Saw it Happen: 1485–1688*. Blackwell.

TINNISWOOD, A. (1993) *Speke Hall: A Resource Book for Teachers*. National Trust.

WAGNER, R. (1926) *Sir Francis Drake's Voyage Around the World: its Aims and Achievements*. Howell, San Francisco.

WITHINGTON, L. (ed.) (1876) *Elizabethan England*. Walter Scott Ltd (includes material from William Harrison's *Chronologie*).

Chapter 6: Victorian Britain

BAMFORD, S. (1972 edition) *Walks in South Lancs and on its Borders*. Harvester Press.

CAM, H. (1961) *Historical Novels*. Historical Association Pamphlet G.48.

CHARLES-EDWARDS, T. and RICHARDSON, B. (1958) *They Saw it Happen: 1689–1897*. Basil Blackwell.

DUFF, D. (1970) *Victoria Travels*. Muller.

GRAY, P. (1995) *The Irish Famine*. Thames & Hudson.

*GREENWOOD, M. (1958) *The Railway Revolution, 1825–45*. Longman.

*HOCKING, S. (1968 edition) *Her Benny*. The Gallery Press, Liverpool.

HORN, S. (1989) *The Victorian and Edwardian Schoolchild*. Alan Sutton.

FRANKUM, W. and LAWRIE, J. (1992) *The Victorian Schoolday* (Katesgrove Primary School, Dorothy Street, Reading, Berks RG1 2NL).

LAWRIE, J. and NOBLE, P. (1990) *Victorian Times*. Unwin Hyman.

*LONGMATE, E. (1980) *Children at Work 1830–85*. Longman.

MARRIOTT, J. (1940) *English History in English Fiction*. Blackie.

NOCK, O. S. (1959) *The Railway Race to the North*. Ian Allen.

**Our Native England* (1885). Walker Smith.

REES, R. and WITHERLEY, J. (1996) *Victorian Britain*. National Trust (about Quarry Bank Mill, Styal, near Wilmslow, Cheshire).

*ROSS, A. (1982) *Going to School*. A. & C. Black.

Chapter 7: Britain Since 1930

*ARDLEY, N. (1989) *How We Build Bridges*. Macmillan.

BUSH, J. (1990) *Moving On: Northamptonshire and a Wider World*. Nene College Publications.

BUTLIN, B. and DACRE, P. (1982) *A Showman to the End*. Robson Books.

CWMBRAN NEW TOWN DEVELOPMENT CORPORATION (1951) *Abridged Report on the Master Plan*.

*DUNN, A. (1983) *Structures: Bridges*. Wayland.

*EVANS, A. (1983) *The Motor Car*. Cambridge History of Mankind Series. Cambridge University Press.

*FOREMAN, M. (1995) *After the War was Over*. Pavilion Books.

PRIESTLEY, J. B. (1994 edition) *English Journey*. Mandarin.

REEVES, F. (1989) *Race and Borough Politics*. Gower.

RIDEN, P. (1988) *Rebuilding a Valley*. Cwmbran Development Corporation.

The *Scotsman* newspaper (2 July 1971).

(For current information about Cwmbran, write to: Director of Development, Torfaen County Borough Council, County Hall, Cwmbran NP44 2WM.)

Chapter 8: Local history

BECK, J. (1969) *Tudor Cheshire*. Cheshire Community Council.

DUNNACHIE, N. (n.d.) *The Turners: Merchants and Manufacturers at Helmshore, Lancs.* (County Museum Service, Higher Mill, Holcombe Road, Helmshore, Rossendale, Lancs BB4 4NP).

GRIFFIN, J. and EDDERSHAW, D. (1997) *Using Local History Sources*. Hodder & Stoughton Educational.

HARRIS, B. E. (1984) 'The Debate on the Rows', *Journal of Cheshire Archaeological Society No. 67*.

HUGHES, J. and G. *The King in the Oak Tree*. Blackwell.

*JAMES, J. (1979) *The Blacksmith's House*. A. & C. Black (using a probate inventory).

KENNETT, A. (1986) *Tudor Chester*. Chester Record Office.

King Charles Preserved (1956) Miniature Books, Rodale Press.

SMITH, J. (ed.) (1996) *Tudor Chester* pack. Cheshire Education, Grosvenor Museum, Chester.

STEPHENS, W. B. (1977) *Teaching Local History*. Manchester University Press.

Teachers' Resources: Tudor and Stuart Times (1992) Ginn. (Stories of Robert Brerewood and of Charles II, pp. 24–8.)

The Unique Rows of Chester (1995) Cheshire County Council.

WEINSTOCK, R. (1994) *Tudor London*. HMSO (p. 25 for illuminated capital of the young Elizabeth I: to be compared with Source 2 and the cover illustration).

Chapter 9: Historical fiction (for children: including some titles relevant to earlier chapters)

*ABRAHAMS, E. (1990) *Tanya Moves House*. Harmony Publishing.

*AVERY, G. (1985) *Ellen's Birthday*. Hamish Hamilton.

*BAKER, J. (1988) *Window*. Walker Books.

*BARNARD, P. (1993) *Escape from the Workhouse*. Anglia Young Books.

*BAWDEN, N. (1973) *Carrie's War*. Puffin.

*BRADMAN, T. and DUPASQUIER, P. (1990) *The Sandal*. Picture Puffins.

*BRIGHTON, C. (1989) *Nijinsky*. Doubleday.

*BRIGHTON, C. (1990) *Mozart*. Frances Lincoln.

*CHILDS, A. (1991) *Under the Rose: A Tudor Spy Story*. Anglia.

*CRESSWELL, H. (1987) *Moondial*. Faber and Faber.

*CROSSLEY-HOLLAND, K. (1982) *Beowulf*. Oxford University Press.

*DEARY, T. (1986) *A Witch in Time*. Corgi Books.

*DE JONG, M. (1956) *The House of Sixty Fathers*. Harper.

*DOHERTY, B. (1986) *Granny was a Buffer Girl*. Lions.

*DOHERTY, B. (1995) *Street Child*. Penguin.

*FLOURNOY, V. (1987) *The Patchwork Quilt*. Picture Puffins.

*FOREMAN, M. (1989) *War Boy*. Pavilion Books.

*FOREMAN, M. (1989) *War Games*. Pavilion Books.

*FOREMAN, M. (1989) *The Boy who Sailed with Columbus*. Pavilion Books.

*FOX, M. (1984) *Wilfrid Gordon McDonald Partridge*. Picture Puffins.

*FRANKLIN WATTS (1996) *Sparks* series (linked to the National Curriculum).

FREEDMAN, R. (1962) *Using Non-Fiction Trade Books in the Elementary Classroom*. NCTEL.

*FRITZ, J. (1991) *The Great Adventures of Christopher Columbus*. Pavilion Books.

*GALLAZ, C. and INNOCENTI, R. (1985) *Rose Blanche*. Jonathan Cape.

*GERRARD, R. (1986) *Sir Francis Drake: His Daring Deeds* and *Matilda Jane*. Gollancz.

*GERRARD, R. (1994) *The Favershams*. Puffin.

*GIBBONS, A. (1991) *The Jaws of the Dragon* and *Whose Side Are You On?*. Dent.

*GIBBONS, A. (1995) *Street of Tall People*. Orion.

*GIBBONS, A. (1995) *Climbing Boys*. Collins.

Ginn History Stories (1994) (following the National Curriculum).

*GODDALL, J. (1978) *The Story of an English Village*. Macmillan.

*GODDALL, J. (1991) *The Great Days of a Country House*. Murray.

*GODDALL, J. (1990) *The Story of the Seaside*. Andre Deutsch.

*GODDALL, J. (1991) *The Story of a Country House*. Murray.

*GODDARD, G. (1994) *Will's First Battle*. Scholastic Publications.

*HOLM, A. (1989) *I Am David*. Mammoth.

*HUCK, C. et al. (1993) *Children's Literature in the Elementary School*. Harcourt Brace.

*HUGHES, S. (1994) *Lucy and Tom's Christmas*. Picture Puffins.

*KAYE, G. (1987) *A Breath of Fresh Air*. Andre Deutsch.

*KERR, J. (1993) *When Hitler Stole Pink Rabbit*. Armada Lions.

*KING-SMITH, D. (1993) *When Hitler Stole Pink Rabbit*. Armada Lions.

*LEWIS, K. (1991) *The Shepherd Boy*. Walker Books.

*LIVELY, P. (1978) *The Ghost of Thomas Kempe*. Heinemann and Piccolo.

*McCRORY, M. and MICHAEL, E. (1989) *Grandmother's Tale*. Magi.

MADDEN, E. (1992) *A Teachers' Guide to Story-Telling at Historical Sites*. English Heritage.

*MASON, A. (1993) *The Children's Atlas of Exploration*. Millbrook.

*MORIMOTO, J. (1987) *My Hiroshima*. Viking.

*MORPURGO, M. (1989) *Waiting for Anya*. Viking.

*MORPURGO, M. (1990) *Friend or Foe?* Mammoth.

*OPPENHEIM, S. (1992) *The Lily Cupboard*. HarperCollins.

*PEARCE, P. (1976) *Tom's Midnight Garden*. Puffin.

*POSTGATE, O. and LINNELL, N. (1991) *Columbus the Triumphant Failure*. Kingfisher.

*POWER, E. and R. (1977 edition) *Boys and Girls of History* and *More Boys and Girls of History*. Dobson (real and imaginary short stories, using sources. Reprint of a pioneering example of 'child's-eye' history).

*REISS, J. (1972) *The Upstairs Room*. Puffin.

*ROSEN, M. and BURRIDGE, J. (1995) *Treasure Islands*. BBC Publications.

*SERRAILLIER, I. (1975) *The Silver Sword*. Puffin.

*SHELDON, D. (1990) *The Whales' Song*. Hutchinson.

*SUTCLIFFE, R. (1963) *Dragon Slayer*. Penguin.

*SUTCLIFFE, R. (1978) *Song for a Dark Queen*. Knight.

*SUTCLIFFE, R. (1977) *Eagle of the Ninth*. Penguin.

*THOMAS, J. R. (1989) *The Princess in the Pig Pen*. Collins.

*TOMLINSON, T. (1989) *The Flither Pickers*. Walker Books.

*TOMLINSON, T. (1989) *Summer Witches*. Julia MacRae.

*TREASE, G. (1995) *No Horn at Midnight*. Macmillan.

*TREASE, G. (1995) *Henry King to Be*. MacDonald Young Books.

*UTTLEY, A. (1977) *A Traveller in Time*. Puffin.

*WALSH, J. (1985) *A Chance Child*. Puffin.

*WESTALL, R. (1975) *The Machine Gunners*. Puffin.

*WESTALL, R. (1994) *A Time of Fire*. Pan Macmillan.

*WESTALL, R. (1994) *Blitz*. Lions.

*WILD, M. and VIVAS, J. (1991) *Let the Celebrations Begin*. Orchard Books.

*YOLEN, J. (1992) *Encounter*. Harcourt, Brace, Jovanovitch.

Chapter 10: Using historical reference books

*ABELLS, C. (1986) *Children We Remember*. Julie MacRae.

BURKE, E. and GLAZER, S. (1994) *Using Non-Fiction in the Classroom*. Scholastic Publications.

CLAIRE, H. (1996) *Reclaiming Our Past: Equality and Diversity in the Primary History Curriculum*. Trentham Books.

HUGHES, P. (1995) *The Greeks: Study Kit*. Scholastic Publications.

HUGHES, P. (1996) *Reading Skills in Context: Key Stage 2*. Folens.

KENYON, J. P. (1992) *A Dictionary of British History*. Wordsworth.

LEMPIÈRE, J. F. (1984) *Classical Dictionary*. Routledge.

MALLETT, H. (1992) *Making Facts Matter*. Paul Chapman.

[SC]MILLS, A. D. (1993) *A Dictionary of English Place-Names*. Oxford University Press.

NATIONAL WRITING PROJECT (1990) *What are Writers Made of?* SCDC/Nelson.

NEATE, B. (1992) *Finding Out About Finding Out*. Hodder & Stoughton Educational.

SUTHERLAND, Z. and ARBUTHNOT, M. (1986) *Children and Books*. Scott, Forsman (USA).

WOOD, S. (1995) 'Writing Up the Past' in *Language and Learning*. Questions Publishing Company.

WRAGG, E. C. and BROWN, G. (1993) *Questioning*. Routledge.

Index